OPPORTUNITIES AND OBSTACLES

A True Biography

Herr Schlegel

Strategic Book Group

Strategic Book Group
P.O. Box 333
Durham CT 06422
www.StrategicBookClub.com

ISBN: 978-1-60860-854-6

Printed in the United States of America

Book Design: Stacie Tingen

Dedications

The Author dedicates this book to his ancestors who stressed dedication and the work ethics. To his wife of almost 60 years who provided the atmosphere for the accomplishments and the many lonely nights for the travel related to his job. To the hundreds who provided the opportunities for excellence, especially Col Solar, Conrad Busse, Ted Olsen and the others who provided the opportunities for excellence and accomplishment

Contents

Introduction

This is the true story of a unique man who always struggled for excellence in every thing he attempted. It includes the successes, dedication and stumbling blocks encountered in the search for excellence. He has received many awards for his efforts and made many friends in the process. He has accomplished many extra tasks, and has maintained the attitudes, ethics, and attributes ingrained by his ancestors. He has maintains that life is a continual learning experience and that any individual should realize this. He shares all of the experiences of over 70 years with the reader for an understanding of the opportunities and roadblocks encountered in the process. He also shares these experiences so that others may be aware of the opportunities and pitfalls to be aware of, and provides recommendations so that the reader can elude the errors he encountered.

He is proud of his accomplishments and the impact he with others have had on technological advances reducing U.S Army, Navy, Marine, and Air Force casualties from the tens of thousands per month to a fraction of those previously, presently estimated to be less than a hundred per month. He has maintained the highest ethical and moral standards that are a model to be followed, despite criticism, backstabbing and other negative factors. He has spent most of his life researching various subjects, including those for Military applications, business possibilities, and participated in many social, professional, fraternal. Civic, and veteran's organizations He is known by many personnel worldwide as a professional.

He never achieved National fame as a politician or criminal and he is proud of the good things he has accomplished and has led others to prosper. Those paying attention to his suggestions and recommendations have done well, and those choosing not to listen to him have faltered.

CHAPTER I

The Early Years

George was born on October 13, 1932, in a log house about 4 miles northwest of a small south central Illinois town. He was known as Eldon until he was married and served in the U.S. Navy. His mother always claimed that he was born on October 11, but his birth certificate reflects October 13. It was just after the Great Depression of 1929, most everyone had nothing, and poor compared to today's standards. The Doctor came to the house in a horse and buggy and delivered him, and his father paid the Doctor with a side of a hog that he had butchered that day. His mother was a teacher, and earned about $250.00 per year [8 months]. He was named after his great-grandfather and a student his mother had as a student that she highly respected. His father worked at any job he could find for fifty cents per day, and saved most of that. Some times he would walk 10 to 20 miles to and from an available job. The most popular among men at that time was to go northward to the "corn country" to shuck corn and throw it into a wagon pulled with horses. His father did this for several years and farmed before George's parents were married on May 17, 1930. His father had saved enough cash to purchase a Ford Model "A" truck.

Just before George was born, his father picked apples, loaded them on his truck and traveled about 60 miles to sell them. That required 3 days, andhe grossed about $70.00. He slept in his truck because there were no Motels where he went and he couldn't afford them anyway. There was a hill on the route that the truck could not go up forward. He had to turn around and back up the hill in reverse gear because the truck had more powcr in reverse than forward. The road was one of the few that was paved at that time. The day before his son was born, his mother asked George's father to stay home, because the baby was ready to be born.

His father had only graduated from the 8th grade, but he was a shrewd livestock, farm equipment and automobile trader, as were his grandfather and great-grandfather. His farther also had the philosophy that, "Anything worth doing is worth doing right the first time." Subsequent to George's birth, he made a decent living by farming and trading livestock. He was also an avid hunter and fisherman, so they always had plenty to eat, warm clothing, shoes and boots, and heat in the winter with wood or coal heaters. He had been associated with his father in a Chevrolet dealership in Argus, Indiana during the mid –twenties and all four brothers and sister would be in sales sometime during their lifetime, and one brother would become a manufacturer of welding products.

George had scarlet fever before he was two years old, and has been told that it was doubtful he would survive. His parents told him that at one time they gave up hope, that he would lay still and not move a muscle.

The earliest thing he remembers is when his mother was teaching at Lacey school, near Farina, IL They were in a 1926 Chevrolet taking his mother to school. The car jerked in ruts of the dirt road, the door became unlatched, and his mother fell out of the car and rolled into the ditch with her lunch bag. Luckily, she was not hurt. She reentered the car, and went on to school. He remembers living in Farina, IL, and his father had rented pasture for livestock he had traded for. He also remembers that they lived in a rural house less than a mile from the school where his mother taught. She had previously roomed at one of the school board members, which was very near the school. She had two of her students in school and their name was Norman. It was customary for teachers to stay at one of the school board members or someone near the school. Most of the roads were dirt, so they were impossible to travel during the winter.

The family always had plenty to eat and as with most rural people, grew all their vegetables, fruits, meats, and nuts. These were fresh in the summer, and canned and preserved for winter meals. They always had heat in the winter from coal or wood and all the clothes they needed, many home-made. They relied on cross- ventilation in summer until they had electricity available from the Rural Electrification Agency [REA] in the thirties. They could then have fans in the summer to cool and in the winter to circulate the heated air. Much of the family clothing was made at home.

They lived in Farina, IL, a house in the country near Farina, and a house north of Xenia, where George's brother was born in 1937. That was at this house north of Xenia that a neighbor came one cold, snowy night, saying he was drunk and wanted to know where George's father was. His mother explained that his father was not home from some sales calls on used cars, but she would tell him when he got home. His father arrived home about an hour later. When his mother told him about the neighbor, the father left immediately to find the neighbor, because he was afraid he would freeze to death. About two hours later, his father returned. He had found the neighbor and took him to his home about 3 miles from their house, which was near a railroad. He said that he opened the door, saw the floor covered with bottles being capped, helped the neighbor into the house, closed the door, and left. George's father was troubled with Asthma, and had to sit backwards in a chair to sleep at night. He saved enough money from farming, and trading automobiles and livestock to buy his first 40 acres about 1938.

A railroad ran through the land, and had a siding switch where rail cars were parked for unloading of limestone, phosphate, potash, and coal. Periodically, sparks from the coal fired train locomotives would burn parts of the 40 acres. His father's uncle was a Brakeman on the Illinois Central railroad, and when they would "switch" to let another train pass or deliver fertilizer, they would visit. It was less than a quarter mile from the home of his Great Grandmother's brother, Thomas Cantrell. Tom had one daughter, Doris who married Tom Newton. Their son Don Newton and George became very close friends throughout their school years, including High School. They even double dated with two girls on several occasions. They built and flew many model airplanes during their early years and even sailed them from Don's barn loft. This was during the change to tractors and power equipment from horse-drawn equipment. It was customary to limit visits, and the mothers would demand that when they told the children one hour, it meant just that. If visits extended over one hour or the established time, the mother would go after the child with a "switch" which was a small limb off a tree or bush.

They had fun playing under an iron bridge near Don's home. One day a car went over the bridge, scared them, and George cut the top of his head when he rose up. The bridge had a wood deck, and was very noisy when a vehicle crossed it. When Don's Father bought a new Farmall "H" tractor and a 42-inch Combine, Don made a working model of the combine. Another pastime they had was grabbing an electric fence with both hands, and see who could hold on to it the longest. Another thing they did, which has never been told, was to urinate on the electric fence.

This was an era when many used tractors with steel wheels, were converted to rubber tires, and changed southern Illinois farming forever. Some farmers kept their steel wheel tractors and farmed with them until they retired, until the 1950's. Earlier George's aunt, who lived in Chicago, told his father that all the warehouses were filled with repossessed cars. He rode a railroad boxcar on the Illinois Central Railroad that ran through their property and directly to Chicago, stayed that night with his sister, then the next morning bought a car and drove it home. It was such a good deal that he could sell the car in one or two days, with a good profit. He did this until he could afford a tow bar and buy two cars at a time. He set up a car lot in Flora, IL, and sold cars from a six-sided cabin on the lot. He later bought another tow bar, hired a driver, and then could transport three at once, and not ride the train anymore. He had a full time mechanic who would make any necessary repairs or repaint the cars.

About this time George remembers going to Chicago on a passenger train to from Effingham, IL visit his aunt Eva, where she took them to the Brookfield zoo and Shedds aquarium. They lived in the house on the first forty acres they had purchased. One morning when he was feeding hogs, he saw his father run around the house and crawl into the window. His father began throwing furniture and clothes out the window. George then saw smoke coming from the roof and then knew what was happening. His mother had been cooking breakfast on a wood-fired cook stove, and the chimney, which was old and made of brick, caught fire. His father had gotten all of their belongings out of the house before the house burned completely. George was very distraught, and his parents sent him to his grandparents house about two and one half miles down the road. He walked the two and half miles crying all the way.

It was at this house about 1938 that his father began buying used tractors and farm equipment from farmers and dealers in Central and Northern Illinois, and reselling them to local farmers. This is what revolutionized the farming in south central Illinois. Many tractors had steel wheels, and many were converted to accommodate rubber tires. Some of the early tractors were; McCormick-Deering 10-20 and 15-30, Farmall F-12, F-14, F-20 and F-30; and John Deere GP, A, B, and G. A welding shop in Flora had a good business cutting off the steel wheels and welding rims on the outside for mounting rubber tires. George would drive all of these tractors before he was 12 years old.

While his father had a used car lot next to the Post Office in Flora, one of the men he had working for him was inducted into the Navy, and was the first from Clay County killed in Pearl Harbor. The Flora American Legion Post was named after the sailor.

George's father bought a limousine with 16 Cylinders that people would not buy because of very low gas mileage, although was very plush. When the lot sold for a lumberyard and he had to vacate the lot, he pulled the six-sided cabin to the farm with the Limousine. He later junked the limousine, and his mother used the upholstery and padding to make coats and bed clothing. He sold the rest for junk, which was in good demand for recycling. When he was on his back under the car disassembling the limousine, he took a bolt out of the spring, and the car fell on him. George became scared, but his father told him to get a jack, told him where to put it, and George raised the car off him, and he crawled out sore but not injured.

George's father was in Chicago buying cars when the weather turned cold and blustery at home. They were out of coal for the heater and cook stove, so George and his mother had to cut wood to burn until they could get more coal. This was sometime in November George was about 6 years old, and adept at using a saw and axe.

It was common for the cousins from Indiana and northern Illinois to go to the farm and visit their grandparents, uncles and aunts, and cousins during the summer.

George's grandmother always had chickens. In the spring, she would purchase 200 small chicks, and raise them for laying hens, and the roosters for dressing, cooking and eating. She planned to have at least 100 laying hens to produce the eggs to sell. Most farm and some small town families also had turkeys, ducks, geese, and guineas. All were sources for meals and special occasions. The eggs were also eaten and used for baking. Nests for the turkey, duck, goose and guineas were often hidden in fencerows, and finding the nests was a challenge for the young children. Both grandmothers also had large gardens as many had at that time. George remembers one time, when his cousin was visiting in the summer the cousin began throwing corncobs at the roosters. The corncobs came from the corn that was fed to hogs and chickens. They would eat the corn off the cob and leave the cobs. This was a common sight on most farms. The cousin was backing up as the roosters approached, and suddenly stepped into a ditch, and fell backward. The roosters jumped on him, and he yelled for help. George's uncle on the other family side operated a hatchery in the local town, and was known as the chicken expert in the area. He would treat the chickens for diseases, and caponize them for producing capons for meat production. Common practice among the farmers was to feed their chickens laying mash, which they purchased at the local feed store. His great uncle Clyde operated a chicken hatchery for several years.

During this time, most children went barefoot in the summer. Most had two pairs of shoes, one for work, and the other for "dress" to wear to church, going to town, etc. At school some wore their work shoes and a few wore their "Sunday" shoes. There were many cut feet, thorns, and minor injuries to these tender bare feet when going barefoot.

During his early years of school he attended the West Ward School in Flora, Florena School south of Flora, White Pine school northwest of Xenia, Center school north of Xenia, Peoria and Mattoon, IL and attended the Xenia Public School and Forest Grove school northwest of Xenia. He also attended Shadden School in Marion County one year where his mother taught there. All students carried their lunch in "dinner buckets' which contained a sandwich, fruit of some kind an a dessert, either pie or cake. The school usually had a pie supper sometime during the year at which the girls would each bake a pie to be auctioned to the highest bidder. The successful bidder then had to eat the pie with the lass who baked it. Also, the ladies would bake cakes for a cakewalk. Money made at these affairs would go for special projects of the school. At these pie suppers, George would talk to the girl he thought the most of, and get the number of her pie. He usually paid a higher bid, but he got to eat the pie with the choice girl of the school. These were large events and many attended that were not connected to the school. At one pie supper, a young man, Bud Hale who was known to drink too much, tried to get others to bet him he could pull the schoolhouse with his car. Needless to say, no one took him up on the bet.

About this time several children would receive a jigsaw puzzle for Christmas and they cherished it, and when friends were visiting it was common to work the puzzle, especially on rainy days or evenings. This was the only puzzle they had, and the worked it over and over. They might get another for the next Christmas, but this was doubtful because they already had one.

Most of the Christmas presents during this period were new clothing, shoes, or something they really needed. The jigsaw puzzle was on of the few they received, because that was not a necessity. There were always toys and most of the time their stockings were stuffed with candy, nuts and an orange.

The land in that area had been depleted by the growing of Red Top hay as a primary source for livestock feed and the seed sold for making dye for all cloth material. George's father bought the land for as little as ten dollars per acre, because most people in that area thought that the land would never grow anything of value.

His father had the soil tested, applied limestone, potash, and phosphate, and began using mixed fertilizer for crops including Soybeans, Corn, Clover, Oats, Wheat, Lespedeza; and selling the grain. This revolutionized the farming practices, along with more modern tractors and equipment.

The spreading of limestone and other fertilizers became a lucrative service for several truckers in the area. George enjoyed all of his Grade School years very much, and they all had a lot of good clean fun. He always had a favorite girl in the class that he liked. He was particularly interested in the math and science subjects. He graduated from the eighth grade at White Pine School in Clay County, IL.

During the early and mid thirties, most roads were unimproved. Most of the rural families traveled in horse drawn wagons and buggies. When they went single, they would usually ride a horse. They would take all day on Saturday to take their eggs and cream to sell, and use the money received to purchase groceries, hardware, feed and other necessary supplies. The families would take their lunch, tie their horses to a hitching rail, feed and water their horses at noontime, and plan to arrive home by sunset. As roads were improved, automobiles and trucks became more plentiful.

All during grade school years, the students all enjoyed their recesses and lunch periods. They all carried their lunch to school, and all students either walked to school or rode bicycles. Distances to school ranged from one-half mile to one and one-fourth miles. They played all sorts of games, including Baseball, Softball, Tag, and Blackman. They didn't have access to any modern playground equipment as known of today. Some other scientific things they did were hunting eggs from frogs, and other reptiles/fish, and crawfish. They collected tree leaves, identified them, and mounted them in a scrapbook. They also learned to identify insects, and study their habits. They put the eggs in the water or environment they came from, and watch them hatch and grow. They gathered frog legs and crawfish tails, which their mothers fried. Today, these are considered delicacies. Most of the boys had bicycles by this time, and would ride them to school when the roads were dry. They also wired bicycles to a battery and Model "T" auto coil, to give the rider a shock when he touched his bicycle. The common dare was to touch the pump handle with their tongue in the wintertime. For those not familiar with this, the tongue would stick to the pump handle or any metal object.

They all had boots, raincoats, caps and other furnishings to wear in bad and cold weather. The teachers in the rural schools had to do their own janitor work. All the schools had a coal bin in a corner room. A large furnace was near the coal bin, and the teacher had to scoop the coal from the bin for the furnace. A local parent and the men on the School Board would keep the lawn mowed, and the School Board members took care of all outside repair and work. Most repairs were done in the summer when the students were on summer vacation. For overnight in cold weather, the teacher would stoke the furnace with larger chunks of coal at night, and close the "damper" so the furnace was ready to start the next morning. The furnaces had a water tank, to keep the humidity at the correct level. They had cloakrooms, one for girls and the other for boys, to hang coats, store boots/overshoes, and stow other necessities during school time. All rural schools were one-room with as little as one student in a grade. Some grades at different times had no students in that grade and had no classes for those grade levels. Each grade had a recital period during the school day. The younger students would learn from the upper grades recitals. They had a small Library, and all had at least one set of Encyclopedias, Dictionaries, World Atlas, pull-down world map sheets as well as U.S. and each State, a World Globe, and several other reference books. The main vehicle for teaching was the blackboard, with chalk of several colors, and erasers.

The schools each had outside toilets, one for the boys, and one for the girls, separated by approximately 100 ft. They both had paths, usually coated with cinders from the furnace. Water came from an outside well with a pump. There was also a water bucket inside during bad weather with a dipper to dip the water. Each student had his/her own cup or folding cup to drink from, either from the pump or from the dipper and water bucket, or later a water can with a faucet.

From the time George was 5 years old, he had tasks, or chores as they were called, to do early in the morning, or before he went to school, and in the evening or when he came home from school. Some of these were milking the cow[s], feeding livestock, watering livestock, taking up eggs from the chicken house, etc. Also he learned at an early age to harness and saddle horses. In the winter they cut Hedge for fence posts, repaired fences, and did other repairs in preparation for spring. His father was an avid hunter, and they and hunted and trapped Mink, Fox, Opossum, Raccoon, etc. Also, they hunted Prairie Chickens, Quail, and pheasants. Prairie chickens would become almost extinct in the future years due to clearing of the fencerows and meadows. They would collect furs, stretched them on a board, and in the Spring, would take them to St. Louis, Mo and sell them to F.C. Taylor Fur Co. His father some way found out when another farmer had livestock for sale. Starting when George was about 8 years old, his father would send him to bring the cow home. He would give him the money to pay for it, and George would walk 4 or 5 miles, put a halter on the cow, and lead her home. At about 9 years old he began driving tractors and operating farm equipment, servicing equipment, and driving trucks in the field. His father purchased a new Ford-Ferguson tractor when George was about 11 years old from an uncle who was a Ford Ferguson tractor dealer in Aurora, IL. His father drove it home, and the trip took two days. Of course he had to obtain a permit to buy it due to the rationing and price controls of World War II, which will be discussed later. The day he arrived with the new tractor, George was plowing with a McCormick-Deering 10-20 with steel wheels. When turning at the end of the field, he would rapidly turn the steering wheel the direction he wanted to turn, locked it with his foot, and stretched back to trip the plow. His father bought a mounted hydraulic plow with the new tractor, and this was a godsend for George. When he was eleven or 12 years old his father purchased a new 60-inch Allis-Chalmers combine to harvest seed with, which was unassembled for shipping. George, and a cousin assembled the combine, and operated it during the entire summer, combining Sweet Clover, Red Clover, Red Top, Wheat, Oats, and Soybeans. They pulled it with the Ford-Ferguson tractor previously purchased, performed all service and repair. On one occasion his father was helping them unclog the combine cylinder, which had clover stems wrapped around it. He was using a knife to cut the stems, when the knife slipped, and cut his leg just above his knee. He had to keep pressure on the wound to reduce bleeding, and his mother had to take his father to the Doctor to get it stitched up.

The older tractors were started with a crank, or flywheel on John Deere tractors. George started these tractors, and serviced the tractors and equipment beginning when he was 10 or 11 years old.

During the late Thirties and early Forties, cigarettes were 10 to 15 cents per pack, gasoline was 12-20 cents per gallon, and chewing gum was a penny per pack. Kerosene for lamps and lanterns was 9 to 12 cents per gallon and eight-ounce soft drinks were five to ten cents per bottle. Haircuts were 25 cents, and the admission to a movie was 10 to 25 cents. They usually had a "hired man" to help with the farm work, which cost about twenty five cents per hour, and when his mother was teaching, they had a "hired girl" to help take care of the house and keep George and his brothers during the school year and summer, and cook lunch for the males at noon. They were provided room and board along with the pay for housework and keeping the children. Some that he remembers were, Geneva Miller, Letha Mulvany, and Ruth Hendrix. Some of the hired men were Charles Whitney, Gene Lane, Leroy Weaver and others he cannot recall. They usually stayed at George's house during the week, and went home to their families for the weekend.

From the time George was about three years old, they would get a "whipping" when they stepped out of line or sassed their parents. Some times, it was a "switch" cut from a tree, a belt or a slap on our "butt." The schools had a wood paddle that was used by the Principal for students that misbehaved in class or during recess or intermission between classes. In other words, any time the students were at the school or riding the school bus. This was used only on the "butt" that hurt their ego more than any-thing else.

Communication during the late thirties and early forties was by bat-tery powered radios; and telephones on which they could call people on their own line, by ringing a combination of "shorts" and "longs." Other calls had to go through an operator, which was called "central". All contact was through operators for local and long distance. The operators knew everyone in the local area, and knew more about what was going on in the community, and more gossip than anyone else, because they listened in on all calls. The men on each line were required to repair the line and provide upkeep for the line. .

Lighting was with kerosene lamps and lanterns. The Aladdin Lamp was the greatest advancement thus far because it emitted much more light than its predecessor. Later, White Gas was used to burn through "mantels" which emitted a whiter and much brighter light. This white gas has advanced to be lantern and camp stove fuel today, but called "Camp Stove Fuel."

Family pastimes were going to a movie, playing Pinochle with friends/neighbors, visiting relatives and neighbors or listening to the radio, and sometimes they would go to his Uncle's house in Flora to listen to the heavyweight boxing matches. They also shelled nuts they had gathered from the woods. People frequently visited relatives, neighbors and friends.

Between 1937 and 1939, the oil boom had hit Clay, Richland and Marion County. Most of the crews came from Texas and Oklahoma. The heads of the crews called drillers were old experienced pros on the oilrigs, and the rest of the crews were called roughnecks. They were mostly, what the term indicated; rough men that worked on the rigs 24 hours per day, seven days per week in 8-hour shifts. When a rig went up, it didn't shut down until the well was completed. They worked in mud and during rain, snow, mud, sleet, and everything. The well servicing crews also were on call 24 hours per day, seven days per week. The trucks beds were made of heavy-duty steel, had winches, and were toughened for rough service. If the site were muddy, they would be pulled through the mud to the site with large bulldozers. It was a common sight to see a bulldozer on site for these purposes.

Again they didn't let anything stop or delay them. Some of the service teams, were Schlumberger, Halliburton and Dowell, who did Electric Logging to locate the oil formation, fracture the well casing with explosives to let the oil flow, cementing the well below the formation and chemical treatments to make the oil flow better. While drilling, samples would be taken frequently, to determine when they reached the oil-bearing formation. The Geologist would stay at the well, and sleep in his vehicle, to analyze the samples, and determine when they reached the oil formation. The Geologists never left the well after the crew reached the designated formation, and supervised the completion of the well. Once the well was completed and casing was installed. If the well was "dry" casing would not be set and a cementer would be called in to plug the well. The rig would be dismantled, and loaded on trucks for transport to the next site. If the well were successful, a "spudder" would be brought in to clean and complete the well.

Many of the crews were heavy drinkers and heavy smokers but hard workers. When they worked they worked hard, and on their off-duty hours gambled, drank liquor, gambled, and played hard at the local bar, and "Cat Houses" scattered all over the small towns. Fights were common when they had disagreements. George remembers going with his parents, and some of their friends to see the red lights all over town in Salem and Flora, signifying that the ladies were available. Most of the workers rented rooms in a local home, and some of the hostesses were the worker's "mistress", and when they were working, the ladies would light the red light, for other customers. The roughnecks made about $4.00 per hour, and the whores charged about $10.00 per visit. There were no time limits. The red light bulbs were stocked at the local hardware stores. Several teenagers worked as roughnecks, and many worked part time in service stations, stores, etc.

Local truckers would collect livestock from the local farmers, and transport them to the stockyards in East St. Louis, IL then go across the river to St. Louis, Mo to pick up supplies for the local merchants. The hotel near the stockyards had a bar, gambling, and women for hire and anything else to get the truckers money. As time went on local men became experienced, and assumed jobs as Drillers and Roughnecks. The cathouses dried up, because local workers replaced the transients and the demand for that service dried up. Most of the local men were family men, and didn't care for the other kinds of pastime and couldn't afford them if they wanted to participate.

Many wonder what happened to the women that operated the cathouses. It was undoubtedly kept secret, and many probably changed their lifestyle and became highly respected ladies of the community in their later years.

In the late thirties, a madman in Germany, Adolph Hitler began his quest to conquer the world. In 1939, he had invaded most of Europe, was attacking Russia on the Eastern Front, was bombarding England, had started taking over Africa and also was executing most Jewish people. This

17

is when President Franklin Roosevelt declared war on Germany and sent troops to North Africa to drive him back. This started World War II.

As the intensity increased, the Selective Service [Draft Boards] was established, drafting young men for Military Service. The fighting forces dominated the news, women began working in Defense Plants, replacing men in building everything from ammunition to airplanes and ships Many men too old for or not suitable the Draft went to these factories and shipyards to work, as far away as Alaska.

On December 5, 1940 George's great-grandmother died. George really loved her, as she always was very nice to him. She had married "Chick" Henninger after his great grandfather had passed away on May 14, 1922 from complications from asthma. She lived in a two-story house in the small town, and every time George and his parents visited her, she would always have some treat for them. She was a sweet small lady and Mr. Henninger was always very friendly. She had kept the farm where she and George's great-grandfather lived. George and his parents rented the farm and house. The house on the farm was built by his great-grandfather, and was a two-story house with a large kitchen. After the great-grandmother's death, the farm was sold to a neighbor, Mr. and Mrs. Horton and their daughter, Ruth who was never married.

The war intensified as the German forces were driven out of North Africa, and through Italy, into Europe. Later, the English and United States Forces landed On Normandy Beach and began driving the Germans back from France. This weakened the German forces on the Eastern Front and the Russians were able to drive the Germans back on the Western front. England suffered heavy losses from the bombardment by the Germans, especially with the V-1 and V-2 Rockets.

On December 7, 1941 the Japanese pulled a surprise attack on forces at Pearl Harbor. The United States was not prepared, but President Roosevelt declared war on Japan. This caused the United States to go on full wartime production. The United States was not prepared to respond adequately. They had one Aircraft Carrier in the Pacific, and it would change positions at night to make the Japanese think that there were more carriers. Pearl Harbor was completely destroyed by their attack. Many young men lost their lives on that dreadful day. Many people were not aware of how unprepared the USA was. Shipbuilders, aircraft factories, ammunition plants, clothing plants, auto factories and others went on 24 hour day, 7 day operations One shipbuilder, Henry J. Kaiser, produced "Liberty Ships" at a unprecedented rate. The Merchant Marines and the Coast Guard were integrated into the U.S. Navy, and all Cruise Ships were used to transport personnel, equipment, and supplies. Several did not make it, and were sunk by German U-Boats, airplanes, and mines in the water. The servicemen didn't have time, or the desire for mind-altering drugs or other activity, which plague the world today.

Back home in the U.S., almost everything was rationed or subject to price-controls. The auto factories ceased production in 1941, to concentrate on military equipment. Rationed items included tires, coffee, sugar, gasoline, oil, and everything of military importance. Farm equipment was only available by certification of need. Price controls were established on many new and used items, including autos, farm equipment, airplanes, trucks, shop equipment, etc. The "Black Market" flourished with only cash transactions on everything that did not require documentation such as a Title. For example an auto was subject to a ceiling price, but loose items could be sold for any price. Other sales were cash only, so the transaction could not be traced. Honey was used as a sugar substitute in ice cream and candy production, as well as other industries requiring sweeteners. All scrap metal was in high demand for the Military, and every one gathered and sold all available scrap metal for reuse in new materials. Everyone was patriotic, and displayed American flags in their homes and on their bicycles and autos. Mothers who had sons or daughters had a flag hanging in their front window, with one or more stars signifying a member or members in the Armed Services. If they had one star, it meant that they had one family member in the Service. George remembers a widowed lady that displayed four stars. There was another color star if the family member was deceased.

The Servicemen came from every line of work and profession. They proved that they were the best in the World, being innovative, worked as teams, and never faltered. Women volunteered as Nurses and clerical personnel. The ones serving from his immediate family were: His uncle who served in the Navy on a LST [Landing Ship, Tank/Troops] in the Pacific; one cousin who served in the Navy; and another cousin served with the Marines in the Pacific. Almost every family was touched by the War, and many gave the ultimate sacrifice.

George's father always had various cars and trucks around, so George drove most of them. The oldest cars he actually drove were Ford Model "T", and Models "A" and "B." George watched the truck drivers intently and noticed the drivers double-clutching when they were shifting gears on trucks with manual gearshifts and 4 speed transmissions.

Germany surrendered when the USA and allies met in Berlin, and when the Atomic Bomb was dropped on Hiroshima, Japan immediately surrendered, due to the mass destruction. All knew when the War was over before the news was received. George and a cousin were driving tractors home from the field, when they heard sirens and train whistles blowing. They both stopped and were taken aghast. They knew that signaled the end of the War. They even danced around the tractors, shouting," The war is over".

Generators, batteries and lights were installed on the early tractors that were not factory equipped for them. They worked from daylight to dark every day usually except Sunday. The later tractors were factory equipped with lights, and the workday became longer in the growing and harvesting seasons.

After the war, those serving came back, some with Foreign brides, went to school/ college on the GI Bill and became very dependable in their professions. They have been called, "The Greatest Generation" by Tom Brokaw.

Many returned with battle scars and injuries that were painful, but they endured, and gave the USA their best. The same was true of those who were Prisoners of War, who suffered torture, many for several years, in the hands of their captors. Many did not survive. The torture was more severe in the hands of the Japanese, than the Germans. The worst in Germany was the Holocaust, in which the German Nazi's systematically destructed over six million European Jewish people before and during World War II. Locally, the veterans obtained jobs as Rural Mail Carriers, because they had a 5-point veterans preference and the disabled ones had a 10-point preference. They were dependable, and some were part time farmers. They would get to the post office to sort the mail at 5:30 or 6:00 AM and had all the mail delivered by about noon. They always were at the same places the same time each day. The ones that had other jobs besides farming worked in the afternoon at their place of employment. They were strong community leaders. However these brave men who returned were and are the proudest to be Americans. Many still would not talk about their experiences, but some were not bothered by their experiences, and talked freely about them.

As mentioned before, the book, "The Greatest Generation", by Tom Brokaw, is excellent reading on this subject.

In 1946, the first automobiles after the war were produced. Some parts were molded from scrap metal. One Chevrolet was damaged in a wreck, and it had the imprint "Coca Cola" in the roof. A Ford Crown Victoria was not involved in a crash, but the top separated in the center, leaving a gaping hole.

The countryside was dotted mostly with small farmers and some workers. George, at various times visited most, some of them relatives. The older ones were, Henry Bennett, Arthur Nugent, Tom Beard, Johnny Davis, Roger Davis, Tom Cantrell, Stanley Warren, Ted Jean, "Ham" Jones, Jeff Smith, Clyde Smith, Willy Wyman, Ross Lane, Walt Jones, Lance Warren, Edgar Tracy, Corbett Anderson, W.A. Slagley, Verl Beard, Leslie Beard, Myrtle Warren, Ira Anderson, Clint Stipp, Myron Anderson, Byron Anderson, Earl Fatheree, John Mason, Lew Anderson, Jim Dillman, Forrest Anderson, Wayne Whitney, Jim McKinney, Asher Anderson, Raleigh Cantrell, Dallas Ruckman, Ed Hockman, Walter Weaver, Lowell Anderson, Lizzie Waggoner, Riley Waggoner, Amy Hartin, Paul Young, Charley McGrew, Emory Thomas, John Boles, John Smith, George Beard, Curt Warren, Asher Smith, Earnest Pribble, Charley Horton, Curt Anderson, Wayne Woodward, Charley Dean, Elbridge Paul, Richard O'Brien, Xon Warren, Wayne Fitzjarrald, Alva Wires, Leslie Anderson, Claude Tate, Thomas O'Brien, Green Cannon, Noel Pickle, Herman Trinkle, and a few more. Most of those homesteads have been demolished, and there are less than 10 of these houses today. Elbridge Paul operated a threshing machine, and threshed hay and grain for most of the farmers. Jim Dillman, a single man living with his parents, worked in the barn loft when they were threshing hay. He always wore a long sleeved shirt, and would pull the hay back from where the hay dropped, and worked there 10 hours per day in dust and chaff when the outside temperature was in the upper 90's.

He never complained, and he was the only one in the area that would take that job.

George had been attending many farm sales with his father. Some always started a "Crap" game in an isolated area. It was not uncommon for the gamblers to appear after something had been sold. One would remark, "Gee, I wanted that, how much did it sell for?"

George graduated from grade school, in the spring of 1946, and registered for Flora High School, then known as Harter-Stanford Township High School. All during grade school, he walked to and from school. In the First Grade, he walked one and a half miles with other students. This was when they lived South of US 50 in Flora, and he attended Florena School, which was further south. He remembers that two of the people he walked with were the Pat and Phyllis Berry, who lived near them. The other schools were closer than this one. They walked in all kinds of weather, and they all had proper clothing and boots/overshoes for bad weather.

CHAPTER II

High School Years

The summer after he graduated from grade school, his father found that a schoolmate from his eighth grade class was the Dean of Engineering at the University of Illinois. He was surprised, as he said this schoolmate was the dumbest student in grade school. He called him, and he invited them to meet with him at his home in Champaign, to discuss George's interest in Engineering. They talked over many things, among them how he ever got to that position. He said that he decided he wanted to be an Engineer, and he set his sights high, and worked as a laborer for 8 years "on the short end of a long handled shovel". He then decided to get an education, and that was what he did. He told George to take all the Math and Science in high school, to prepare for Engineering school, and if he decided on the University of Illinois, he would help him any way he could, or if he didn't attend college, the Math and Science would help him in anything he wanted to do. .

One of the courses George registered for was Agriculture. The school hired a new "Ag" teacher, Mr. Zimmerman. Before school started, he visited the students welcoming them to his class, and inviting the students to join the Future Farmers of America [FFA]. George found out later that by joining this FFA Chapter, he was one of the Charter members of this Chapter. He was elected to one of the offices, played on the basketball team, had FFA Projects which he had to keep records of the project progress, associated costs, and year-end closeout. George had previously had 4-H projects on which he kept records. George's project was a plot of land of their farm, on which he followed the advice as to fertilizer, type of seed, and care of the crop through harvest. Mr. Zimmerman would visit during the year, to see the progress, and offer advice. The "Ag" department had a shop area, which he enjoyed, learning welding, woodwork and machinery maintenance and service. It was in the "AG" shop George built a wagon bed to haul grain at their farm. George had no way of knowing then that his nephew Doug would be the head of the "Ag" dept and FFA almost fifty years later. The wagon George built was used on the farm for many years afterward.

Throughout high school, he took all the Math and Science courses available, because he had the reputation of being an expert in operation and repair of farm equipment, trucks and autos. Also his aptitude test reflected high mathematical and mechanical ability. He still had his sights on an engineering career. He also took English, Typing, Shop, and Spanish.

He had a lot of fun during high school, developed many friends, and had no aspirations to do anything but farm and trade farm equipment and livestock. He dated several girls during these four years. Most of the entertainment was Movies, Roller Rink Skating, Hayrides, and other small parties, driving around on Sunday afternoon, visiting friends and relatives and Church gatherings. The girls, as well as their mothers surely had a lot of respect for him, as he had as the utmost respect for them. They had no distractions that developed in the latter part of the Century. No one had any problems with alcohol, drugs abuse or other criminal activity. Of course they had their spats, but these were settled with a fistfight, or a wrestling bout. Most of them had no time for mischief, because they had to work evenings and during vacation. These long hours only permitted dating on Saturday nights and Sunday afternoon. A couple could go to a movie, stop for a hamburger and French fries on less than $2.00, not counting gas for the two. A letter sent to anywhere in the U.S. cost 3 cents, and a Post Card cost one cent to send. A haircut cost 35 to 50 cents.

During High School, he seldom studied outside school hours. He just wanted to get by with reasonable grades, with the least effort necessary. On the farm, he repaired all vehicles, tractors and farm equipment, including cleaning and repainting, and attended auctions with his father.

He reached his fifteenth birthday in October 1947, passed his driver test the first time, and received his driver license. He had been driving trucks, cars and tractors since he was 12. In 1947 his cousin, Don's father bought a new Frazer Manhattan automobile. This was the most elegant post war automobile, and they dated together in this and whatever vehicle George's family had available. Don had received his driver license in February 1947 before George received his in October. At first George had a 1936 Ford that had to be pushed or pulled to start. Driving the eight miles and to Flora and return, it would use one gallon of gas and two gallons of oil. Not much of a car, but they had a lot of fun with it. Next, George owned a 1937 Chevrolet, which was a good auto. In 1948 his father purchased a new Kaiser Deluxe which was a model of the Kaiser-Frazer Corp, the same Company that Don's father purchased his Frazer Manhattan the year before. Henry Kaiser, one of the founders, had built the Liberty Ships during World War II, faster and more responsive than ever thought possible. The Tucker, the most advanced auto of that time, was to be built in 1948, but for some reason it was never available. It was front wheel drive, and some of the other features made it too advanced for that era. There were a few prototypes that sold, and they soon became collector's keepsakes.

Also during high school, he had a 1947 Plymouth Club Coupe, with which he had a lot of enjoyment and pleasure. In this era, the average auto was considered to last about 50,000 miles before a major overhaul, or being worn out. It was unusual for an auto to last up to 100,000 miles. Tires had to be replaced about every 10,000 miles.

The first year or two of high school, the roads were not all improved. During this time his family lived about 3 miles from the school bus stop. A contractor was improving the main road during this time. Sometimes George and other friends had to walk to the bus stop or home in the evening, when the road was almost impassable. They would leave their boots and coveralls at what was called the Town House, which was a Township polling place. It was about 15 ft by 25 ft, and had outdoor toilets. This was the school bus stop. Later, after the road was improved, the school bus ran to about ½ mile from his house. White Pine school was on the corner where the school bus stopped. During inclement weather, they could get shelter on the schoolhouse porch. He seldom drove a car to school, only on special occasions. It was common for them, several years before during the winter, to see autos left at an improved road, and walk to their home on unimproved roads.

In 1947 they bought a 140-acre farm about one mile from the Town House, where the bus stopped before the main road was improved. After the road was improved [gravel] the walk to the school bus was only 1/4 mile. Even after obtaining their driver license, the students only drove a car to school for special occasions. However, George made several trips with their 2-ton truck to the coalmines of Southern Illinois to purchase coal for the family's heating and cooking. He also made several trips with the truck to limestone quarries about 20 miles from their home to haul rock to spread on their lane to the house, which was ¼ mile off the main road. He operated a combine and in the evening after sunset he hauled the grain to the grain elevators, and sometimes due to the long lines to dump, he returned home after midnight. He had been using double clutching when switching gears on the 2-ton truck to avoid gear grinding. Many of the trucks had a two-speed axle in addition to the regular 4-speeds. This gave the driver 8 speeds forward and two in reverse.

On April 9, 1948 George's parents received a call that his mother's father had died suddenly. He had retired from school teaching and was a real estate broker. He was showing a client a farm they were interested in and became stuck in the mud road. He and the lady's husband got out to push the car, with the lady in the car to drive. When they began to push, George's grandfather dropped dead from a heart failure. He had taught the 8th grade at Flora for about 25 years, and had been the principal at a grade school in Pekin, Illinois. They kept their house in Flora, and returned when he retired from the job at Pekin. George had stayed at their house the winter of his freshman year at the high school in Flora and prepared all his own meals, clothes washing and ironing.

The only high school courses he had trouble with were: Typing and English in his Junior and Senior years. The rest came easy. During one class cancellation, he took Spanish and General Shop.

On September 16, 1950 George's grandfather on his father's side passed away at the State Hospital at Alton. He had been sent there on two occasions because he would wander off and neighbors would take him home, because he couldn't remember where he was. On a few occasions George's father would go looking for him. He had retired when he was in his upper 40's and the main thing he would do after 1948 was sit in a rocking chair just inside his front door and constantly smoked a pipe with Prince Albert tobacco for many years. He had about a hundred of old Prince Albert cans stored in his barn. All the family attended the funeral, and that was one of the few times they were all together. George's grandmother stayed at the home place for a while, then his father took her to California to reside with her only daughter. She later was homesick, and the only way she could get home was to fly on an airliner. That was the first time she had flown, and dearly loved the trip. She later returned to California where she died.

George did not attend the Senior Prom because he and his date didn't know how to dance. They dressed for the prom, but went to the drive-in movie instead. He graduated in May 1950, still not knowing what he wanted to do for a career, but the idea of Engineering remained on his mind. In1950, he and his father traded their autos for new Plymouths. The list price on his father's car was $1330.00. He had a 1949 Plymouth to trade in. The one George bought was listed for $1280.00. He traded the 1947 Plymouth for his. After graduation, he farmed with his father, and was not serious about anything else. In the fall 1950 he went on a hayride and saw a girl that he had known for several years, but had not dated. She looked lonely and he was also lonely, so they sat together the rest of the evening. This started off and on dating during the ensuing months. He was torn between two girls that he thought a lot of until the spring of 1951, when he decided that the one that he was on the hayride with was the one he was most interested in. When he asked her to marry him, she said that she would have to ask her Mother. The next date, she said her mother said it was ok and at Baccalaureate on a Sunday in May, he gave her an engagement ring. They then set the date of June 17, 1951 to be married. At that point his family lived in town, two bocks from her family.

Shortly after that, her mother called George's mother to find out what they had planned. That's when the mothers got into the act in preparation for the wedding, and that was probably a good thing, because it may not have been consummated without them. Her father had purchased a new Chevrolet for her, but told her that if she got married that she would not get it. He had planned for her to go to college. He kept in the garage and would not even let her drive it. After the wedding he sold it.

They started remodeling a farmhouse of his father's to start housekeeping at. On June 17they were married, the first to be married in the new Methodist Church, accompanied by his cousin and her husband, Betty and Oren Mulvany, who were the last to be married in the old church before it was torn down for the new one to be built. Incidentally, Oren was a cousin of George's on another side of the family. Kathryn's Father was the one that organized building of the new Church and Kathryn had attended church there most of her life. At the wedding, Oren asked him for the ring. George had forgotten it, and had to run home [one block], and get it.   Only their families and close relatives were at the wedding. They were, of course, both of their parents, his two brothers, his Grandmother Smith, Kathryn's Grandmother, his cousin Melba Smith, and Betty and Oren Mulvany who were their attendants.

At this point they had the house ready to move into. They left after the wedding and stopped their first night at Mattoon, IL, then on to visit two of his Uncles in Sandwich, IL. They had told no one where they were going, because they didn't know themselves. They then went back home to the house they had ready for occupancy. George and Kathryn were named the sponsors for the Methodist Youth Fellowship at the church they were married in. They had a fine group of young people and thoroughly enjoyed this task. George's youngest brother was one of the youth that attended regularly. From all indications, the youth were elated to have them as sponsors.

The Korean War was on, and some people got married and immediately had a baby to escape the Draft. Some young men went to Canada to escape the Draft. They were in no hurry as this was not their primary purpose for getting married.

They had the usual when they returned, tin cans under their bed, and a surprise charivari and shower shortly thereafter. George got thrown in the pond near their house, and they had refreshments, and received many gifts, some useful, and some as a joke. The farming season was upon them, and he worked hard that summer and fall. In the late Fall, they moved to another country house owned by his wife's father. He had bought 10 acres from Kathryn's aunt, and had a F-30 Farmall tractor, with other implements. While plowing the 10 acres, there was an old well that he didn't know about. The front end of the tractor fell into the well, and came to a sudden stop. The impact threw him over the steering wheel, which he was holding onto firmly. The front of the tractor broke off, front wheels and all. He found a used front end, and replaced it. The next thing he did was to fill in the well. When researching the Title for the 10 acres, Since Kathryn's Aunt, who was the owner at one time, he found she had a daughter, and he had to get her former husband to sign a deed over to him, because of his Dowry rights. He got an earful from him on the aunt, but has never told anyone of the incident or the comments he made to George. She never told that she had any children from that husband. He does know she that she hated men for some reason or other. She never remarried, and always resided with one or more women.

One afternoon, George stopped by his parents' house, and they were not at home. He waited about an hour, and returned. They were home then, and his father told him that his mother had collapsed on the porch, and had gone to bed to rest. He also told George that she had been passing blood, and was very weak. George talked to her, and told her she had to go to the hospital. She didn't argue with him. She dressed and his dad and he helped her into George's car and proceeded to Flora, where they stopped at George's brother's house to tell him they were going to the hospital in Olney. When George got onto their porch, he looked back and his mother was behind him just starting up the steps. She collapsed on the steps, and they helped her into the house. George called a Funeral home owner, and asked him to take her to Olney in his ambulance. They followed the ambulance to Olney. When she arrived, she went into the emergency room, and they immediately started to give her blood. She had to stay there several days. The Doctor told them that she was lucky, that she had a bleeding ulcer and her veins were ready to collapse because of lack of blood, and if they had been 10 minutes longer, they could not have saved her. After that was healed, she had a hip replacement due to Arthritis.

On October 8, 1951 George's last remaining great-grandfather passed away at his son's house in Xenia IL. He had lived a good life after his wife had passed away in 1929. It was not known and probably never will be known whether she accidentally fell in the well or deliberately jumped in the well. It was well known that she was mentally unstable. He had moved to town and had a good friend that owned an auto, and they really enjoyed going different places including church. When he got sick his son insisted he occupy a bedroom at the son's house where he died. George was with him during his last moments.

That Winter George and Kathryn took his cousin, Melba with them to New Orleans to visit Kathryn's aunt and their family. Then they went to the Tampa, FL area to visit his uncle and his family. They were in no hurry, but George had talked to the Navy Recruiter before, as no company would hire him because he was Draft age. When he returned, his father told him that the Draft Board clerk had been calling, and passed the word for George to contact her as soon as he returned.

George went to the Draft Board office, and the Navy Recruiter was there. He asked him if he was ready to enlist. George hesitated and glanced over to the Draft Board clerk. She showed him the letter to report for the draft and said she had been holding it for a week, but it had to go out if he chose not to enlist. He made the decision to enlist in the Navy, and signed the enlistment papers. The recruiter gave him train tickets and a instruction sheet where to go in St. Louis and told him to be at the Railroad Station at about 4:00AM the next day, February 20, 1952. The next morning Kathryn took him to the Station, and he went to St. Louis for induction.

He spent all day February 20,1952 taking tests and physicals to verify that he was suitable for Military Service. It was here that he learned what a "short-arm" inspection was. That evening, they boarded a Troop train, bound for San Diego, CA for "Boot Camp". Kathryn and a friend were at the Depot in St Louis to see George off. It was all Navy recruits, so they picked up additional train cars along the way and at Kansas City, MO and Denver, CO where they were put on a siding waiting for trains from other parts of the Country. It was daybreak when he realized they were in the railroad yard, waiting. About 9:00 AM they started moving again. It would take them more than two days to get to San Diego, and when they arrived they found that there were recruits from all parts of the United States on that train.

CHAPTER III

U.S. Navy

When they arrived in San Diego, Navy busses picked them up from the train station, and transported them the Naval Training Center. They saw sailors marching with rifles, and George was so naïve that he didn't know the Navy carried or drilled with rifles. This was one of the first of many surprises, and he would have over the next several weeks. First, the Navy referred the rifles the sailors were carrying as "Pieces". George found that he would sleep with the piece on the side of his bed at night, and march with it all day. During classes, they would stack the pieces in order, and recover them for the march to the next class. When they arrived, the first task was the haircut, which lasted 30 seconds, and would result in a burr haircut for everyone. The barbers would jokingly ask the recruit how he wanted his haircut Then the haircut was what the Navy wanted, not what the recruit wanted. Then came the clothing issue, which was also a fast production line. The issuers would look at the recruits, guess their sizes, and gather all the clothing [uniforms that they would wear for the next 11 weeks], from shorts and tee shirts to shoes and socks, both blue wool and white uniforms, blue denim work uniforms, white hats, blue dress hat, pea coat, Navy handbook, Sea bag and all. They were then marched to their barracks to stow their clothing in the lockers. They immediately changed from their civilian clothes, and packed them in boxes to be sent back home. A Chief Petty Officer was assigned to each Company. George's Company was 52-184, and their Chief's' name was Royce. They were told which uniform to wear each day. This first training was called "Boot Camp", which was designed to break everyone down to the same level, and then teach Navy subjects and tradition, and mold them for Military discipline and courtesy. The men from the rural areas seemed to endure better than their city counterparts. Each morning the plan of the day was posted, and it was followed very closely.

The first 4 weeks they would drill 7 days a week, 12 hours per day, have no "Liberty" and purchases at the Navy Exchange store were prohibited. The obese ones would lose weight, and the slender ones would gain weight. For every meal, they were given allocated portions, and were directed to eat everything on their tray, they punished if anyone left any part of it and seconds were not allowed. They had classes every day, washed, dried, and folded or rolled the clothing and had a standard layout to store it in their lockers. They would have surprise inspections, when they had to lay all their clothing on their bunk in a certain array, rolled, tied with "Clothes stops" and any errors were dealt with harassment, and extra duty. Also as mentioned before, they would live with their piece 24 hours per day and 7days per week, tied on their bunk at night and carried on their shoulder at all other times, except during classes, when they had a particular method to stack them.

They soon learned the navy slang. Pogey Food was candy, nuts and other snack food. Pogey Bait was any young lass who was under the age of 16 years. The mass hall was called the "Slop Chute." The Ship's Store was where they bought clothing, luggage and almost everything but groceries. The Grocery store was the Commissary.

This Boot Camp was the utmost in discipline and harassment resulting in the unfit being weeded out, and others being mentally affected. Almost everyone, at various times, would wish they were not there. Kathryn had started working at the local Shoe Factory, because George thought he would have 4 years duty on a ship. However, this would change drastically over the next several months. First, he would have his first "Liberty" after the fourth week, and he wrote to Kathryn about coming to San Diego on that weekend, because he was lonely. Some Recruits on their first Liberty got Tattoos, drank their first Beer, and got "laid." She rented a room from a sister of a friend in Xenia, and he visited her on one day each weekend. There were some times that she could go to the Visitor Center on the Base, and he was allowed to visit with her in the evening during the week, and when he had "Duty".

They practiced shipboard tasks on a mock-up of a Navy Destroyer, which was called the "USS Never Sail." They were also taught the tasks of participating in" Landing party" which was for invasion of a hostile environment. The Navy had frequent swimming classes for the recruits, and all were required to pass the swimming tests before graduating from Boot Camp.

After several weeks, they were transferred to Camp Elliot, in the mountains, which was previously a Marine Training Center, for 4 weeks of intense training and aptitude testing. They were taught survival techniques and had to pass another swimming test to graduate from Boot Camp.

They returned to the Naval Training Center at San Diego for the last week. At the end of Boot Camp, The "Billets" were posted, which told them where they would be assigned. Every one was anxious to see what their next assignment would be. George's assignment, along with several others, was to the Naval Air Technical Training Center at Norman, Oklahoma for "P' school which was a primary Aviation school, to be followed by Aviation Machinist "A" School. He didn't realize then that this would change his life and career forever. Kathryn returned to Illinois, and George went to Norman, OK. The recruits were on a troop train from San Diego to Oklahoma City, Oklahoma, where they spent the night in a hotel.

The next day, they took a Taxi to Norman and reported in at the Naval Air Technical Training Center [NATTC] at Norman, OK June 9, 1952, and during the orientation George learned that they could live off base and draw what the Navy called "Commuted Rations". He called Kathryn and told her that he would find a furnished apartment and for her to plan to join him, because he would be there until November 1952. George and a good friend, Mr. Chapman, from North Carolina, decided they would find a two-bedroom apartment. He and his wife would share the apartment and each would share the expenses half and half. They found an upstairs two-bedroom apartment, and the owner lived on the ground level. It was only one-half block from the University of Oklahoma football practice field. George had "Duty" on either Saturday or Sunday every other weekend. They really enjoyed their stay there, watching the University of Oklahoma football team practice and taking drives into the countryside and to Northern Texas. In the country, there was a new road being built, and there were many rose rocks along the side of the road. They collected several, because they had never seen these before. They would be lifetime keepsakes, after they learned the history of the rocks.

The first part was the Basic Airman School. They were taught the basics of Naval Aviation. Navy Chief Petty Officers {E7}, the top Enlisted rank then, taught the courses. They were all very experienced and were never hesitant to share their experiences. They all marched to classes. At this time George was classified as an Airman Apprentice. {E2}. Here they practiced extinguishing aircraft fires, rescuing the crews, etc. It was interesting to learn that foam was and still is used to extinguish aircraft fires and anything that contained any type of oil. Water was and is still useless for these type fires. They also learned to fire all guns and cannons, both in aircraft and on aircraft carriers. This phase contained all the basics of Naval Aviation.

On August 1, 1952, at the end of the Basic Airman course, Mr. Chapman was transferred to Jacksonville, Fl for Aviation Electrician "A" School. George and several others would remain at the NATTC for Aviation Machinist "A" school, from August 4, 1952 to November 7, 1952. They needed to find a less expensive apartment, so they rented an upstairs one-bedroom apartment, two blocks from the entrance to The University of Oklahoma. Kathryn found a job at a Five and Dime store just outside the University, less than two blocks from their apartment. While there, a classmate invited them to their apartment nearby. He had been bragging about his big wife that beat him and kept him in line. He was 6ft 8in tall and slender. When they arrived at their apartment for coffee, a little girl about 4ft 8in answered the door. George didn't know to ask for her husband or her father. During his hesitation, he asked for the friend by first name. She laughed and said, "My husband has been talking too much as usual. I am his wife, and don't believe everything he has told you". She was a very nice lady, and they really enjoyed their acquaintance with them until they left in November.

Also during this time, George traded his 1950 Plymouth for a 1952 Chevrolet Club Coupe. At school, their classes consisted mostly of working on Navy aircraft and engines, in the hanger and in shops. This was very enjoyable, since George had been interested in Aviation since early childhood. One student was directed to change the cold oil return line on a Navy F-6. Several had the same assignment. He yelled, "Hey, Chief. I got the wrong damn line" and oil drained onto the deck [floor] of the hanger. The Chief yelled back, "What the hell do you think this is, a Mack truck? Get a bucket and some rags and clean it up!" That incident never occurred again. They changed many components, including engine cylinders. oil-rings, bearings, oil and fuel pumps, ignition parts including adjusting and changing components, propellers and their pitch-change mechanisms, and all phases of repair, adjusting, calibration and operation of every part of various models of aircraft, engines, and components. They received classroom training on these subjects before working on the aircraft. One incident he remembers, the First Class Petty Officer, {E6} that was their leader in "P" school was observed marching with the "Brig" Company, with the imprint of his First Class Chevron in his sleeve. He had been "Busted" to a basic Airman, {E3}, allegedly, for falsifying muster reports. This was an example of the Navy discipline during this era. They were also grilled on crash survival in aircraft accidents, and continued swimming tests, extinguishing crash fires, as well as rescuing pilots and crewmembers. They also fired larger guns that were carried on Aircraft Carriers, including a 3 inch 50 Caliber Cannon.

When the assignments came out, George, with several others were assigned to Helicopter Anti-Submarine Squadron Three, (HS-3) at Weeksville, NC. None of them had ever heard of Weeksville, NC, so they resorted to maps to locate it. They had 14 days of leave en route and George was promoted to Airman, {E3}. Kathryn and he packed up and headed to Clay County. Other friends from the Trenton, and Belleville IL area, who were assigned to the same Squadron, agreed that they would pick George up for the trip to North Carolina after their 14-day leave was up. They were Rich Fritz, Ray Bruenig, and Norm Kauffman.

They arrived at the Navy Aviation facility Weeksville, NC at 9:15 PM on November 23, 1952, after driving straight through from Illinois. They had left real early, and when they reached West Virginia, they ran into snow and ice. George thinks Ray Bruenig was driving and as they went up in altitude in the mountains on packed snow and ice, their speed kept decreasing as they approached the top of the Allegheny, they stopped because they could go no further without spinning out. A State Highway truck saw their plight, and offered to pull them to the top of the mountain. After they got to the top, it was all down hill from that point. They unhooked from the Highway truck, and stopped in a small town, where they bought the last pair of tire chains the store had. They installed them and continued. After about ten miles, they ran out of the snow and ice, and removed the chains.

When they arrived at the base, they entered the gate that had a guard who, after they showed him their orders, pointed to a large hangar, and said, "HS-3 is in that hangar. Go to the second street on your left, turn left and follow that street. The duty office is at the middle or the hanger, and you will see the parking lot, and the lighted office." They checked in with the Duty Officer in the hangar and asked him where the Helicopters were, because as they later found out this was the largest wood hanger in the world, originally built for Blimps. He pointed to the corner of the hanger to two Bell training helicopters. He told them the squadron had just been organized, and the Anti-submarine helicopters had not arrived yet. They also had a TBM, which was called the 'Turkey Bomber" and a F-4U Corsair fighter. There were two large steel hangers on the Base, which housed two blimp squadrons, used for anti-submarine patrol.

After they checked in at the Squadron, they were directed to the Base duty officer, who assigned them to the Transient Barracks for that night. This was now about 10:30 P.M., and they were very tired. The next day was taken up in getting assigned to permanent quarters, getting chow passes, and getting additional uniforms they needed, from the "Ships Store" and orientation. Their work Uniform was blue dungarees, light blue long-sleeved shirt, work shoes and of course white hats. George went home for the Holidays and around the first of January returned to North Carolina with Kathryn.

When they arrived in North Carolina they rented a furnished apartment in Elizabeth City. The elderly landlord lived in the front part of the house and the couple upstairs were Cletus and Johnnie Gibson. He was a Navy storekeeper at Base Supply and they became good friends.

It was here that George got interested in flying and becoming what was called "Operational Air Crewman". During the first few months he worked on various details, and then was assigned to the Tool Room, with another sailor named Young, from Oregon, They stocked and issued special tools and equipment, and assembled tool boxes for the aircraft maintenance crews. This was a good assignment, as George learned all the special tools needed for the aircraft they had. Later, the Squadron received some HUP-2 [Army equivalent of H-25]. It had been previously used for Search and Rescue.

After installing the Sonar equipment, it was found that the HUP-2 was underpowered, and they encountered failure problems with the engines. They stripped one down for a test, taking off all the weight possible, including the tail fin. They flew this HUP-2 for several hours to evaluate its suitability. One day the control tower called to the hanger to tell the Squadron that they had lost part of the tail on one of their aircraft. Nevertheless, this Helicopter proved useless for their mission. They then began receiving Marine HRS helicopters, the equivalent of the Army H-19 and Navy HO4S. The difference was that the skin on the HRS was Magnesium and the HO4S had aluminum skin. This proved useful, and George was assigned as Second Mechanic, with a sailor named Feller as plane captain, on one of the crews. This was a big step, because he would draw extra flight pay for flying as a crewmember two or four hours per month. The flight pay was called "Flight Skins" and they were either half, which required two hours per month, or full which required four hours flying. They took their HRS on board the carrier, Gilbert Islands in October, 1953 for four weeks of Anti-Submarine Warfare training, along with a AF Fixed wing Antisubmarine Squadron from Norfolk VA, and a rescue

HUP-2 from Lakehurst, NJ. While on the carrier, every night they had to clean the aircraft with hydraulic oil to remove the salt and coat the surface, because the skin was Magnesium, and the salt would erode the skin if not removed. The rotor blades were also washed and coated with hydraulic oil, because the salt spray made the controls sloppy and the blades heavier. The Chief Petty Officer in charge was Chief Lemon. One night he came to the hanger deck where some of the crew were washing the salt water off the HRS, and noticed a Sonar operator not participating in the operation. The Chief asked why he wasn't participating. The Sonar operator replied that he was a Sonar man, and the Chief didn't have the authority to require him to clean the aircraft. The Chief rolled his sleeves up and replied, "By God, you come behind this aircraft, and I will show the authority!" The Sonar operator picked up a bucket and rag, and got busy. They encountered a storm in the Atlantic, and the waves had broken the "Curtains" on the hanger deck, and ruined some of their spare parts stored in the elevator well. Also some of their aircraft were damaged by the waves coming over the flight deck. The Carrier went into New York harbor, passing the Statue Of Liberty, and set anchor in the harbor for repairs. While there, 3 or 4 of them went ashore in New York City. They visited the Empire State Building and toured Times Square. They also had dinner at two of the finest restaurants around Times Square. During the storm, George went up to the sick bay, and asked for some seasick pills. This was the beginning of the storm, and he was one of the first to ask for the pills. They were confined to sleeping quarters, and as the carrier rolled one way, his shoes would slide from his bunk to the lockers about 3 feet away, he would reach to pull them back, and the same routine for each sway.

Also during this cruise, Edward R. Murrow, the well known Newscaster brought a camera crew on board to film the combined ASW operations, and he interviewed some of the crewmen to show on the TV Program, "See it Now". George would see this film several years later at the Naval Reserve base in Memphis, TN. On the carrier, they had one mechanic they nicknamed "Taper Pin". When the rotor blades were folded, they were secured with a tapered pin. The pin had to be removed with a soft hammer, and if the mechanics were not careful, the pin would come out suddenly, and drop to the ground or into the ocean. On several occasions, when he removed the pin, he would rap it hard with the rawhide hammer, and the pin would fly over the side and into the ocean. So many were lost, that all the spare pins became depleted, and they had to have some more flown to the carrier. George was offered a ride in the mail run in a fixed wing airplane. He declined, because he had no desire to be launched by the Catapult, nor to land on that small postage stamp and depend on the Tail Hook and the arresting cables to stop them. They returned the last week in November, and disembarked from the Gilbert Islands at Norfolk, VA.

To qualify as an Air crewman, George had to get a complete physical checkup. When he went to the Dental office, a Hospital Corpsman, Herb Kolb, who was in the same Boot Camp Company, [52-184] at San Diego. The dentist determined that he had some wisdom teeth that needed to be pulled. As he prepared to pull the first one, his pick slipped and lodged in the upper part of George's mouth. He was the roughest dentist George had ever encountered, and he pulled his arm back and clenched his fist, with no intention of hitting the Dentist, but Herb grabbed his arm and said, "No, George, you better not."

George also passed the test and received a Navy drivers license, for anything the squadron had, including forklift, gas truck, and all trucks up to 10-ton tractor and trailer. He passed the tests the first time, because he had driven almost everything on the farm. The tractor was an Auto-Car Diesel, and the trailer was a 40 ft Low Boy. He made several trips to Norfolk, VA to deliver spare parts and equipment for aircraft loading onto a Carrier.

In the meantime George passed the test the first time and was promoted to Third class Petty Officer [E-4] on Nov 16, 1953, and qualified to be a "Plane Captain" or in other words, the crew leader of that aircraft.

One Saturday he was on duty when the squadron began receiving the new HO4S helicopters. George asked the Maintenance Chief if he could have that one. It would be marked as HW 13. The chief told him that he could have it if he would assemble a crew and do the Acceptance Check that weekend. He picked a real eager second mechanic, Charlie Bradshaw, and they completed the check that weekend. With this, he was assigned as an Air crewman and eligible for full flight pay.

Charlie frequently talked about his girlfriend, Barbara, who he said he was going to marry. Almost everyone in the squadron loved Barbara, although they had not met her.

While at this Squadron, George was required to stand watch in the hangar and surrounding area. He carried a 45-caliber pistol, because the material classified as "Secret" was stored in the corner of the hanger. One night he saw the small corner door open, and a uniformed officer enter. He yelled for the officer to halt twice, and he kept coming, without saying a word, George pulled his 45, inserted the clip, and the intruder suddenly stopped and verbally told him who he was. George kept his gun out, and told the intruder to accompany him to the Duty Office. George followed him, giving him instructions on where to go. They entered the Duty Office, and told the intruder to show his identification. The Squadron Duty Officer came in and verified the intruder's identification. The Duty Officer asked him what he was doing on in the area, and he said he was checking the area for security. The Duty Officer told him he was lucky he didn't get shot. The intruder turned to George, and said, "You had your gun loaded, but you would have not shot, would you?" George replied, "If you had not stopped, I would have fired at you". He turned to the Duty Officer, and said, "He wouldn't, would he? The Duty Officer said, "You're damn right he would have. That is what he was told to do, and you would have been the loser. Let this be a lesson, if you want to check us, you come into the main entrance and identify yourself. Don't try to sneak around and tantalize my men." As a Petty Officer Third Class, George was put on a list to for Shore Patrol duty.

George and Kathryn bought a 23 ft Whitley trailer and moved into it at a trailer park north of Elizabeth City NC. It was in a temporary spot at the side of an apartment, just to the rear of the owner's house. George came home one evening, and noticed an Illinois auto parked at the apartment. He asked Kathryn if she knew the people were that moved into the apartment. She told him that their name was Rohde, and that his wife was from Flora, and that she remembered George from high school. This was a joyous reunion, and they would become good friends for many years. He was a Navy flight officer, assigned to one of the ZP (blimp) squadrons at NAF Weeksville. They finally moved the trailer to a permanent space in the center of the park. There was a washhouse and bathrooms in a building in the rear of the park. The trailer had no bath in it, so George installed a toilet in the rear corner, made a cabinet for it, and connected the water line, and ran the sewer drain line to the kitchen drain. They also bought their first TV set, black and white which was the only TV then, and had a 20 ft antenna that would reach about 4 stations. The TV was about a 13 inch, and the cost used was about $300.00. While they were there a Hurricane came through. George checked out Aircraft Tie-downs from the squadron, and tied their trailer down. They were up all night with some friends, and the rain was ferocious. They had some high winds, but the trailer just shook. When the eye arrived, their friends thought it was all over. The TV antenna had broken one guy wire, and the antenna was weaving around. Their friend thought they could go out and secure the antenna during the lull. They hurried out and let the antenna down. About the time they returned to the trailer, the storm hit again, so they weathered out the remainder of the night. Then everything settled down, and they got back to normal, with little damage.

Of course they had their incidents at HS-3. One individual driving the gas truck during night flying operations, lit his lighter to see how much fuel he had in the tank, and yes, it blew up! He had his eyebrows singed, and hair singed, but he jumped into the gas truck and drove it away from the aircraft. He got a commendation for saving the aircraft. He had been in the Navy for something like 18 years, and had been "busted" more times than most sailors had been promoted.

One pilot flew the TBM one day with several crewmembers on board. When he came in to land, he had trouble getting the aircraft on the ground. He made three passes, and on first almost clipped the trees at the end of the runway. On the last pass, He started his approach and brought it down farther down the runway, the crash crew was on site, and he finally got it stopped near the end of the runway. The passengers exited the TBM they and were scared speechless. The TBM was towed to the parking area, and secured. The pilot said he had to clean up, because he "Filled his pants" on that landing. An old First Class Aviation Machinist, who chewed tobacco continually, asked the pilot, "Sir, had you been using the autopilot on this flight?" The pilot replied that he had. The First Class asked if he turned the autopilot off before landing. The Pilot said, " Of course!" The First Class asked the pilot to come with him to the aircraft with him. They crawled up to the cockpit, and the First Class pointed to the autopilot switch, and said, "See, Sir, the switch is still on!" [This pilot was the one labeled as "Dilbert"].

Later, another of their crews were practicing Sonar dips of the coast of Virginia Beach, VA The HO4S lost power and landed on the salt water. The crew exited in their one-man life rafts with no injuries. The aircraft was re-covered, and it was found that the pilot forgot to switch fuel tanks. The fuel selector was on the empty tank. This was the same pilot that had the landing problem with the TBM, and that was nicknamed "Dilbert". The engine had to be replaced, because the salt water had deteriorated the magnesium castings of the engine.

January 1954, George started on extra duty as a "Shore Patrolman." He would get the day off, then report for Shore Patrol at 6:00 PM [1800 hrs Navy time], and return about 1:00AM [0100hrs Navy time] to go home or to the Barracks. On one occasion, they were tasked to help the Sheriff close up a bar that had gambling inside and was serving drinks to minors. The Sheriff told George to watch the door and the bar while the Sheriff Department searched area and destroyed the gambling equipment. The Sheriff told George, "Stay near the front door and watch the waitresses eyes. If you see them light up, you better dodge because she is going to do something." George watched the eyes of the waitress, and he saw them light up, as she was calling him all kinds of foul names. He saw her hand ease toward a beer pitcher, and he "ducked" as the pitcher sailed over his head, hit the wall, and shattered. A Deputy grabbed the waitress and hand-cuffed her.

There were two blimp squadrons on the opposite side of the base in the other very large metal hanger. They were slow, and required several men to hold lines to them before flight and when they landed. It was not unusual for them to spend many hours in the air. When they landed, they were attached to a large boom that attached to the nose before the "linemen" could release the lines.

On one mission, a blimp had refueled from a carrier and returned to base with 80 feet of hose, because a gust of wind caught the blimp while re-fueling at the tanker ship, and it became airborne. On one occasion, while they were returning to base, they spent 8 hours making no ground speed, because they had a strong headwind.

Charlie and George took their HO4S with some others in February 1954, on board the carrier Antietam for 8 weeks of anti-submarine operation in the Caribbean, staging out of Guantanamo Bay, Cuba, commonly referred to as "Gitmo." This was one of the first carriers with a canted deck They also had fixed wing AF Type Anti-Submarine Warfare [ASW] aircraft from Norfolk, VA, and a HUP-2 rescue helicopter from Lakehurst, NJ. The HUP-2 would fly Plane Guard during launching and retrieval of airplanes from the carrier. Kathryn had gone home to Xenia, IL during this operation and the prior deployment on 4 weeks on the Gilbert Islands, to visit their parents and other relatives and friends.

To board the Antietam, the crew flew their HO4S to Quonset Point, RI Naval Air Station. On the way, they encountered low fuel pressure on one aircraft, and landed at Chincoteague VA Naval Air Station. George checked the fuel pump and tried to adjust it, but to no avail. They were dressed in Frog Suits, which were exposure suits, because the water they were to fly over was less than 60 degrees. He went to the base Supply and asked if they had a replacement fuel pump. They did not, but told him they had one for a R-2600. Since their engine was a R-1300, by the same manufacturer, he asked to see it. The only difference was a fitting, so he told the storekeeper that he would try it. He changed the fitting and installed the new fuel pump, adjusted the pressure, and it worked fine. George returned the old fuel pump to supply, and they were on the way again.

It was almost dark when they reached Floyd Bennett Field, New York City, so they spent the night there, where they were assigned to the transient barracks. That night two crewmen from another crew went out barhopping in the area. In the wee hours of the morning, they were attempting to walk back to the field, when one had to urinate. There was no place, so he walked to the center of Flatbush Ave, and did his job. They couldn't find the field, so they hailed a Taxi. The Taxi driver told them he would take them to the barracks for four dollars each. They crawled into the Taxi, went four blocks, and the driver told them they were there. They were in front of the barracks. They knew they had been ripped off, but there was nothing they could do about it.

The next morning it was COLD, minus 8 degrees below Zero. George had lost all his keys, so he had to obtain a lock cutter, and cut locks on the helicopter door, his toolbox and his Sea bag. They went to the hangar and towed the helicopters out to the ramp. They had difficulty starting the engines due to the cold weather, but finally they started. He had the Frog Suit on and the pilots had to run the engines for more than 30 minutes before the oil reached the proper temperature. He was almost frozen when the oil temperature reached the acceptable temperature for operation. They flew over Rockaway beach and Long Island to the carrier at Quonset Point, RI. George was napping, and the pilot called him on the intercom. George didn't answer promptly and the pilot "dropped" the helicopter. George awoke quickly, and the pilot laughed and said, "That will teach you, won't it?" As they approached the Carrier, it looked like a postage stamp in the middle of the ocean. When they arrived on the carrier, the Maintenance Officer found out about the fuel pump, and grounded the helicopter until another fuel pump could be obtained and installed.

While they were on the Antietam, which would sail to the Caribbean Sea and be operating from Guantanamo Naval Base in Cuba, they would conduct operations, including simulated Nuclear attack during the week, and go into Port for the weekend. They had Navy Evaluation Teams, who were not Navy Aviators to accompany them at sea, and they would return with them to the Port on Friday afternoon.

One time on the return, the HUP-2 was preparing to transport the team to shore. The mechanic on the right hand side had trouble getting hold-down reel removed, the pilot tried to take off, and the Helicopter flipped on the right side and rotor blades splintered all over the Carrier deck. None of the Team or the crew was injured, and when the Team was told that another Helicopter would be there shortly, the Team Leader, said, "To hell with the helicopter-We'll take a boat."

They spent one weekend in Port Au Prince, Haiti. The local children would swim out to the ship and beg for anything, or come to them in what was called "Bum boats." The Sailors each had one day to tour Port Au Prince, Haiti. Like Cuba, the people were very poor, and Port Au Prince was lined with many various shops. The Taxicabs were old American models, and at an intersection the first on the horn had the right-of-way

They spent the other weekends at Guantanamo Bay Naval Base, most of the "liberty" was spent on the base, where they would go to the Ship Store, and the NCO and Officer Clubs. One weekend, the only time the City Of Guantanamo had been open to Servicemen, [and to his knowledge, it has not been open since], they visited the city of Guantanamo The train was the vintage of the old, wild, West. The seats were wood, and the backs folded over to the seat on the rear, so the occupant could face in either direction. Along the way, the terrain was swampy, had huts built up on stilts, and the children ran through the water and shouted, "Hey, Joe, give me a nickel!" when one would throw a coin out, if the child didn't catch it and it went into the dirty water, he would dive in and come up with the coin between his teeth and say, "See, Joe, I got it!"

When they arrived in Guantanamo City, beggars swamped them for anything of value. One friend took his expensive camera, watch, and rings, despite warnings by the Navy. All of his belongings were gone in an instant, about 30 seconds, and he didn't see who got them. The city was very poor, and for each block they walked 7 or 8 prostitutes or pimps would proposition them, and some that were not over 8 years old "pimping" for their sister or mother. That was an experience George will never forget.

One day the squadron got a call from the Base, that a Bacardi child from Santiago, Cuba had been kidnapped by a troublemaker by the name of Fidel Castro, and they asked the carrier to send 2 helicopters to rescue the child They told the crews the location of the terrorist camp, and two helicopters went on the search, with crewmembers armed. When they arrived on the scene, the rebels took a couple of shots at them, then as they approached where the child was being held, a crewman fired a couple of shots in return. Then the captor released the child and ran, and the crew landed, grabbed the child, and rapidly took off. They radioed to base and informed them that they had the child, and asked for further instructions. They were told to head to Santiago, and the parents would meet them at the Santiago Airport. The pilots were dressed in flight suits, and the crews were dressed in Flight Deck clothing.

When they arrived in Santiago the parents were there in a Limousine. Mr. Bacardi was the Vice President of Bacardi Distilling Co. It was almost dark, so Mr. Bacardi told them he wanted them to spend the night. They were put up in the finest Hotel in Santiago, treated with their choice of dinner, and told them they could have anything they wanted that night. Remember all the clothes the crews had was their Flight uniforms. The next morning, they had a large breakfast, and were transported out to the airfield in a limousine. Mr. Bacardi had provided the guards for the helicopters all night. The crews then returned to the Carrier, were debriefed, and resumed ASW operations. An account of this episode appeared in Real Magazine about a month later.

During these eight weeks, and during the four weeks on the Gilbert Islands, they did not lose any personnel, but one or two fixed-wing AF aircraft lost power on takeoff from the carrier catapult, and sank into the ocean. All crewmembers escaped and were picked up by the HUP rescue helicopter. The Destroyer Escort [DE] hurried to the rescue, but the rescue helicopter was in the air during all launch and recovery operations. If the DE rescued any carrier personnel, the carrier was required to furnish ice cream to the DE crew, because the DE did not carry ice cream at sea due to space limitations.

The carrier returned to Norfolk, VA in April 1954 to disembark, and the HS-3 crews flew the 50 miles south to Weeksville Naval Air Facility to resume normal training operations. It was common when they returned from deployment the crews had hundreds on cartons of cigarettes loaded in the baggage area of the helicopters. They were purchased on the ship where there was no tax, so instead of 25 or 30 cents per pack, the ones from the ship cost 70 to 80 cents per carton of ten packs.

The squadron had a Lt. Commander H.P. Brown, the Maintenance Officer, who had a twin brother who was the Maintenance Officer at Norfolk, VA. They were identical, and he was nicknamed "Horsepower." One Sailor, Pete Moore, was at Norfolk one day and he said, "Hello, Horsepower" and patted him on the back. The LCDR turned around and asked him, "Who the hell are you?" They both then laughed and the LCDR said, "You must be from HS-3 and think I am your maintenance officer. I am his identical twin, and I can understand your error." Pete went home one morning, upon the advice of another shipmate and found his wife in bed with another man. He walked in, didn't say a word, dumped her purse out on the kitchen table, took everything valuable, and started to leave. His wife by then was dressed, and begged him to not kill them. He quietly told her to get out and left. He went back about three hours later and she and her belongings were gone. Also an Ensign was talking to LCDR Brown about flying, and had a difference of opinion. The Ensign asked him how come he knew anything about flying. The LCDR patted him on the back and replied, "Son, when you get over 10,000 hours, including over 2000 hours of combat, come talk to me." He was one that had the option after World II, to keep his Commission and lose his flying status; or downgraded to Enlisted [First Class or Chief Petty Officer] and retaining his flying status. The Navy had several of these Enlisted Pilots. They also had two Chief Petty Officers [E-7] who were survivors of the Bataan Death March and earned the Medal of Honor during World War II.

George and Charlie kept the helicopter, HW 13 in tip-top condition, and maintained 100 % availability. Shortly after the return, a list for possible to transfer to "Shore" Duty was posted. HS-3 was considered "Preferred Sea Duty." Choices for 3rd class Petty Officers were Pensacola, FL, Corpus Christi, TX or Jacksonville, FL. George was alerted to be transferred to the carrier in the Mediterranean Sea to replace a sick sailor from HS-3 between the times the billets were posted and the assignment arrived. George received notification that he would be transferred to Pensacola, FL, and the assignment to the Mediterranean Sea was cancelled. His orders, dated July 9, 1954 gave him travel time and 18 days leave. He installed a heavy-duty trailer hitch on his Chevrolet; installed electric brakes, and overload springs that he had borrowed from his father. It was a far cry from the trailer hookups known today. The electric brake was manual, that was, to energize the brakes, he had to push a lever on the brake control.

He hooked to the trailer and headed for Pensacola, Fl. Of course there were no Interstate Highways then, so it was all two-lane roads, and somewhat rough. When the trailer started to sway, or bounce, he found that he could tap the brake control, and it would settle down. At some times, the front of the car was lifted off the road. The first day, he made it to Statesboro, Georgia, where he found a hotel about sunset. He stayed there overnight and arrived in Pensacola about dusk the next day. He found a trailer park at 5040 North Palafox St., North of Pensacola, FL, pulled in and rented a space, got the clothes he needed on leave, unhooked the trailer, and headed for Illinois. He left about sunset.

He headed for US Route 45 in Mississippi. He reached Waynesboro, MS, when he got sleepy and pulled over in front of a motel, and went to sleep in his car. He awoke the next morning when the Sun came up, and continued to Illinois. After his leave, he took Kathryn back to Pensacola.

On August 6, George checked in at the Headquarters, U.S. Naval Air Basic Training, at the Naval Air Station at Pensacola. He was checked in at 1435 Hrs [2:35 P.M.]. He was interviewed relative to his preference and experience. He was reassigned to Helicopter Training Unit [HTU-1] at Ellyson Field because he was trained and experienced with helicopters. He left the Naval Air Station at 1600 Hrs. [4:00PM] and was to report to Ellyson Field not later than 2000 Hrs {8:00 PM} He checked in at Ellyson Field about 1900 hrs {7:00 pm., then went home for the night.

The first week was spent on orientation, in-processing, etc. He found another trailer park, the Pecan Grove trailer park at 1717 north "T" street, in the Brownsville section of Pensacola, FL. The spaces were nestled among many large Pecan trees, was well kept, quiet and clean. While there he recoated the trailer roof and painted the exterior light green on the upper section, and dark green on the lower section. It had been light gray on the upper part, and darker gray on the lower portion. He also built a storage shed behind the trailer for tools, etc.

Back at Ellyson Field, he was assigned to the Rotor Shop, where they repaired wood and fiberglass blades, balanced the rotors [both tail and main]. They also replaced bearings, replaced and adjusted pitch links. In July 1955, he was promoted to AD-2 {E-5}, after passing the test the first time.

For a while, the Officers would sponsor a beer party for all officers and enlisted men each Friday afternoon at a picnic area by the water. After one of these parties, a Chief Petty Officer "buzzed" the gate guard with his auto at 60 miles per hour. The Shore Patrol chased him down and arrested him. When he got to the security office, the Duty officer called the Base Commander, and the Commander came to the Duty Office. When he entered the office, he greeted the "prisoner", and said; "What the hell have you been up to now, Benny?" He saw that The Chief had a little too much to drink, and offered to take him home. The duty officer was stunned at the attention the Chief was getting, and asked the Commander why he was so easy on him. The Commander took the Duty Officer to another room, and said, "Benny is a survivor of the Bataan death march, and has a Medal of Honor. It takes an act of Congress to even arrest him, let alone subject him to punishment. I suggest you understand this."

On another occasion, there were twins that were both First Class Aviation Machinists. They were from Southern Illinois, and very capable. One afternoon as one was going home for the evening his auto was hit by a train at an unguarded crossing on Brent Lane and he was killed immediately. This was a Base disaster, and the beer parties stopped.

Kathryn's father and mother from Illinois traveled to Pensacola, FL in the fall of 1984. That was the first and last time her parents would ever see the beaches. They went on the scenic route between Pensacola and Fort Walton, FL and stopped at a motel for the night. George's parents, with brothers Bob and Bill also visited them at Pensacola in 1955.

Kathryn obtained a job with Mrs. Holland, the wife of the park manager, who was the bookkeeper for her brother, who owned the C.N Mason Construction Co. on Pace Boulevard.

On March 17, 1955 Mr. Holland, owner of the park, came to their trailer about 6:30 in the morning to tell them he had just received a telephone call that Kathryn's Father had passed away. There were only two telephones in the park. One was in Mr. Holland's trailer and the other in the washroom. He and Mrs. Holland took Kathryn to their trailer while George went to Ellyson Field to get 15 days emergency Leave. As soon as he returned to the trailer park, they packed and drove nonstop to Illinois.

George worked in the Rotor shop for a few months, and then was selected for transfer to the Advanced Training [HUP-2] Flight Line. The HUP-2 was a larger two-rotor Helicopter, made by Piasaki Helicopters. There were 16 of them that flew with all student solo flights. Before he had been flying with students on the Primary Training Flight Line, in HTK and HTL smaller helicopters. The HTK was a small Helicopter with intermeshing rotors, made by Kaman Helicopters, and the HTL was the standard made by Bell Helicopter, with one Main Rotor and a small rotor on the rear for directional control. The ones selected for flying with students were called the "Sweet sixteen" because there were sixteen of them and they were selected for their flying ability, and knowledge of the helicopters. When they weren't flying, they assisted in scheduling and assisting the HUP line dispatcher.

They were not required to perform duty, and were thoroughly orientated by the Instructors on flying and emergency procedures. They each received full flight pay, but instead being required to fly at least 4 hours per month, they flew 60 to 70 hours per month, flying in the Co-Pilot seat. One aspect of their functions was to perform lifting operations with sandbags with another crewmember. If a student was good, they would let him lift one of them as a live load. Another aspect was to watch the rotor and engine RPM to make sure that the needles were "Married" before takeoff, and maintained all during flight. Also a critical element was "Over speed" during auto-rotation when the engine RPM needle would approach a dangerous level before being brought back to "Idle" when the Collective control was pushed downward. Also, the Rotor speed had to be maintained. If this occurred, it required the helicopter to be grounded at once. On one occasion, George was watching the instruments with a Marine Colonel, when he noticed an engine over speed. He advised the student that he had an over speed on his last autorotation. During an autorotation, the engine is reduced to idle, but the rotor speed must be maintained. Some students were not alert enough to back the throttle off as the pitch was being reduced to let the rotor blades rotate at a safe speed and get the engine to "Idle". He denied it, and George told him that he preferred to remain on the ground if he was going to continue. The student then asked George what to do, and he told him to call the Base, and request a check crew to come to the field where they were operating, and pull the engine sump plug to check for metal particles. The crew came out and removed the sump plug. The mechanic showed it to the pilot, and asked him if he still wanted to operate. The magnetic plug was covered with large particles of metal. The pilot said no, and he did not know the seriousness of an over speed. They then waited for a tow tractor to come after the helicopter, and tow it back to Ellyson Field, where the engine had to be replaced. The Marine Colonel then thanked George for his attentiveness.

The "sweet sixteen" were frequently asked if they wanted to fly the helicopter. If a student flew well, they would take the controls for a while. If he had trouble passing his check-rides or didn't fly well, they would refuse to take the controls. The crewmember could tell at the start-up how good the student was. The Instructors took each of the "sweet sixteen" on check rides, and taught them how to handle any emergency.

On another incident, a student froze on an autorotation, forcing George to override him and land the helicopter safely. The student flew very well, and George had taken the controls during the flight and gave the student suggestions on how to perform auto-rotations and approaches well. Another time, to make a 90 degree left bank, they had to go right 270 degrees The student asked him what he thought was wrong, and George told him the helicopter had came out of check the night before, and the flight control rigging had probably slipped. The student told him, in his own words, "Take this son-of –a- bitch, you know more about what is going on than I do." George took the controls, and asked the student to do the calling on the radio that they were coming in on what was called a "Deferred emergency." George eased in on the approach, where the fire truck and rescue personnel were waiting at the end of the runway. The Base Commander was also there. George eased the helicopter down and landed beside the emergency personnel. The Base Commander came to the helicopter after the rotors shut down. He asked the student who was flying the helicopter, and the student replied, "I am the pilot." The Commander looked at George and said, "Bull shit. I know that George brought it in." They exited the helicopter, and the Commander told George to come to his office immediately. George thought that his career was over, that he was in real trouble.

George went directly to the commander's office, so nervous he could hardly talk, he asked the Secretary to see the Commander as he requested. She said, "Go on in, he is expecting you." As he entered the Commander's office, the Commander greeted George and told him to shut the door. After the door was closed, he put his hand on George's shoulder, and said, "Thanks, George for averting a possible disaster." The Commander told him that he had to discipline him because too many people saw him flying in to the base. At this point, George thought he had the course. The Commander replied, "I am grounding you for 24 hours. Nothing will be inserted in your record and then you go back and continue the outstanding job you are doing." George replied, "Thank you lots, Sir. I sure appreciate your trust in me." During some flights, George was asked by some Senior Officers, (Navy Captain, Marine Colonel) why he did not enter the NAVCAD program. He told them that there were two reasons. One was he didn't have two years college and the other that he was married. They replied that George had outstanding talent and they would like to see him as a Naval Aviation Officer. They gave George their business cards, and told him that if he ever changed his mind, they would get him waivers for the lack of college, and marital status.

George stayed on this assignment for several months. In the early Fall of 1955, Kathryn was pregnant with their first child. They decided that it would be better for her to go to their family doctor in Flora. He sold their trailer to a friend, M.F. Henke, at the base, for $200.00 more than they paid for it in 1953. George took her to Illinois, and moved into the barracks. He was then assigned to the Night Check crew. They would arrive at 4:00 PM [1600 hrs], and work until Midnight or until all the checks were performed and repairs needed for the next day's flying. Right after he started on the Night Check crew, two of them were going to the mess hall to eat lunch one day, when they noticed smoke billowing from opposite of the hanger. They ran over there, because they knew something was wrong. When they got around the hanger, they saw the most horrible scene. Two helicopters had collided in mid-air and caught on fire.

Previously, two Marine Captains had gone to Atlantic City, NJ to escort the Miss America contestants. One of these Captains landed and grabbed the only apparent survivor. Put him in his HUP-2, and headed for the hospital at NAS Pensacola. It was later found out that this injured pilot was the other Captain that had gone to Atlantic City with him. The remains of the other three pilots/students were gathered up and taken to the Morgue at the hospital on Ellyson Field. When the Marine Captain returned to Ellyson, he told the sailors that he knew his friend was dead when he put him in his helicopter. The smell was the worst George ever experienced. He and several other sailors had to put out the fire, and after it cooled, clean it up. Several became sick at the scene, and had to withdraw from it. One helicopter had attempted a take-off, and the other had attempted to land in the same spot. Both were in their "Blind Spots", where they could not see each other. George, after working all afternoon helping clean up the crash, reported for the night check crew at 1600 hrs [4:00 PM].

Another incident happened during a flight demonstration in front of the Headquarters Building for some senior Navy and Marine Corps officers. The HUP-2 was brought in on a sidewise slip landing, and the pilot rolled it too much, and the rotor blades struck the ground. The blades were wood, and splinters scattered all over. The pilot got out without a scratch, but it was embarrassing for the Base Commander. While George was on the night check crew, he would frequently think about what he had done the night before, and would arise early, go to the hangar, and double check what he had done. One critical aspect was safety wire, and he wanted to make sure that he had done it properly before the daily flights started.

The Squadron was requested for an Armed Forces Day demonstration at Natchez, MS. in May 1955. The pilot selected was Lt. Bache, an instructor, a Navy Air Cadet, named John Tucker, from St Louis, Mo and George as the plane captain [crew chief]. Cadet Tucker was the son of the St. Louis MO Mayor. They all got commendations for the demonstration from the Navy Reserve Commander.

While at Ellyson, George was detailed to Shore Patrol on several occasions, and for one month he was to the Master-At-Arms for the barracks. This included management of cleaning, maintenance, and maintaining order in the barracks. He found that some girls would call the Duty Office, and carry on long conversations with whoever answered the phone. They were rough talking, used vulgar language in an attempt to tantalize the sailors into a date and sex. It was thought that marrying a Sailor was their goal, because of the security and income, especially the Officers and Cadets

The Squadron was requested to participate in Hurricane evacuation in Central America in the fall of 1955. They sent four helicopters for this mission. On one occasion there, the crew took off with 6 passengers, and landed with 7 passengers. A baby was born during the flight.

The doctor told Kathryn that she could expect delivery sometime during the last of January 1956. She went home to Illinois in November 1955, and George moved into the Barracks. About Christmas, the night check crew was getting back to the base when they saw Shore Patrol and an Ambulance at the Chief Petty Officers Quarters. When they got into the Barracks, they asked what had happened. They were told that a Chief cook, had no family, had been despondent with the holidays coming up, and he had been drinking heavily and was on some type of medication. He put a pistol to his head and pulled the trigger, before any shipmates could stop him. George had 17 days leave to take before his Discharge, so he scheduled it for January 23, through February 9. He drove straight to Illinois.

On January 26, 1956 they were at Kathryn's mothers house. At 4:30 AM Kathryn awoke with her water breaking. And labor pains starting. George dressed, and her mother was so excited that she couldn't wait for them to get to the hospital. The weather was foggy, and he had to look out the side window to see the road. It was about 10 miles to the hospital. When they got there she went to the delivery room and the nurse called the doctor. George thought they were in for a long wait, and when the nurse told him to get lost, he went to the waiting room to finish his night's sleep on a sofa. He had barely dozed off when the Doctor shook him and told him they had a baby boy, and everything was fine. They discussed the name their son was going to get. After discussion, they decided that they wanted a name that was simple and easy to remember, Dale Allen.

After 3 days he took Kathryn and Dale home to Kathryn's mother's home, and since everything was going fine, he returned to Ellyson Field on Feb 7, 1956, to save a few says leave to get paid for at his discharge, on February 17, 1956.

George's parents built a new ranch, three-bedroom, one-bath house, with an attached two-car garage, on land they owned near the Center school on the main road. This was the best and only new house they ever owned. Several years later, it burned from an unknown cause.

The night of February 16, the squadron gave a farewell party for the ones getting discharged, which lasted until after midnight. George and the others being discharged went back to the barracks and overslept the next morning. They were about an hour late to the Out-Processing Center at the Pensacola NAS. The paymaster looked at them and told them that they didn't have to explain. Again, George drove straight to Illinois non-stop.

That year, he farmed, saved about $3000.00 and they lived in a house that Kathryn's mother had bought. George still wanted college education, so in the fall he applied to Parks College of St Louis University, in Cahokia, IL, in the Aerospace Engineering Curriculum. He had earned the Veterans Benefits program, so in January 1957 Kathryn's mother sold the house and took a trailer in trade. They purchased the trailer and moved it to Viner's trailer court in Cahokia, IL. George had requested active Naval Air Reserve Duty training to make some extra money for college. There they met Doral Miner, who was also a student at Parks and his family, and were friends for many years afterward.

He was assigned to Naval Reserve air transport squadron at, VR-922 NAS St. Louis, MO in December 1956. He qualified for Flight Engineer, and had drills one weekend per month, which paid four days pay per weekend, including flight pay. As flight engineer, on aircraft with two or more engines, he was responsible for all engine functioning from start-up through shutdown. He sat at the engine control panel to the rear of the cockpit, which had all engine gauges and controls including fuel quantity and pressure, oil pressure, manifold pressure, fuel mixture, magneto switches, RPM, etc. The flight engineer was busiest on start-up and in takeoff and emergencies, and during flight he would switch to train other technicians on the panel. On one occasion, the crew was flying over southern Illinois in a R5D [C-54 equivalent] when they encountered a thunderstorm. They could not get clearance to go around the storm, and they were flying at 12,000 feet altitude, and the storm was much higher. This was over the 10,000 ft maximum without using oxygen. Oxygen was not carried on these aircraft, so the pilot told George, "We have to fly through the thunderstorm because we can't go over it. You keep the engines running while I concentrate on keeping this airplane right side up." In 1957, he passed the test and was promoted to First Class Petty Officer, ADR-1 {E-6}, and shortly thereafter the Squadron was disbanded. He went to NAS Olathe, KS to a Naval Reserve Fighter Jet Squadron [VA-881] F-2 Banshee Attack Squadron. One weekend was enough in this Squadron, because he could not fly, and was bored with just flight line duties. He then transferred to another Transport Squadron [VR-732] at NAS Glenview, near Chicago, IL for a few weekends, where they also flew in R-5D transports. On January 23, 1959, George, and several of his friends at St Louis transferred to Patrol Squadron VP-793 at NAS Memphis, TN where they flew the P2V, a two-engine patrol bomber, with the similar flight engineer panel.

They sold the trailer and moved to a house in City View subdivision in Cahokia, IL. They made the change because they needed more room. They sold the trailer to a neighbor in Cahokia. Kathryn worked at Pet Milk Co. in St. Louis, Mo., and rode with others who worked in the same area in St. Louis.

At the end of the first year, 3 Trimesters at Parks, Kathryn's Mother, who had been keeping Dale while Kathryn worked and he went to college, had to return to Xenia to help care for Kathryn's grandmother, who had Cancer. George had exhausted their savings, and had to go back to the farm. He worked hard that year, and his father bought an Allis-Chalmers dealership at Taylorville, IL. George helped with that business, and after harvest in the fall he went back to St. Louis looking for a job. He found a house, moved, and he started at Brown Shoe Co. as a Lab Technician. He was assigned to testing of all shoe materials for quality and durability. Here he met a Vice President of Brown Shoe Co, and also a mixer of latex at that plant. The vice President and "Benny" had started at Brown Shoe Co the same day in the shipping Department, and they knew each other. Benny was still mixing latex as he had done for about 25 years. George also worked with a Real Estate Broker in Belleville. He passed the Broker test the first time, and received his Real Estate Broker's License. After a few months at Brown Shoe Co., he got a call from McDonnell Aircraft Co. in St Louis to come for an interview. Several of his friends in the Navy Reserve also worked there. His interview was with Jack Groff a former Personnel Officer in the Navy at Pensacola, FL who George remembered and he recognized George. In March 1969, He was hired as a Technical Writer, in the Test Division. Here he took project officer's reports, and prepared formal test reports, to forward to the Air Force and Navy, on new aircraft [F-101 and F-4} on contract with McDonnell. In his Reserve Unit, they were receiving shots for active service in Panama. There was a Chief [E-7] Petty Officer that George knew that worked for the Army, and jokingly asked if they had any good jobs open. He replied that there were indeed some jobs open, and that George should go downtown and get a SF-171, send it in and wait.

From June13 to June 29 1959 George spent two weeks of active duty with the Naval Air Reserve Squadron VP-793, at Los Alamitos, CA, for Anti-Submarine Warfare [ASW] aircrew training. This was a very enjoyable experience, although he had been flying in the P2V as Flight Engineer at VP-793 since January 1959. This qualified him to also fly as Radar operator, MAD/Sonobuoy operator and Bombardier.

Meanwhile, he was attending night school at Belleville Area College, taking subjects in Accounting, Psychology, Sociology, etc.

CHAPTER IV

Federal Service And Education

In July 1959 George received call to go to the Army Transportation and Supply Command, at the Mart Building, 12th and Spruce Sts., St Louis, Mo for interviews. He was qualified for a GS-9, but accepted a GS-7 in the Directorate of Maintenance, H-19 Project office at $4980.00 per year. Here, he wrote/revised specifications and publications, Product Improvement, Unsatisfactory Reports, Engineering Change Proposals and technical data. He was considered an expert on the H-19, the Army version of the Navy HO4-S. They rented a small house at 1853 Doris Avenue in Cahokia, IL. He crossed the Mississippi River every day on the McArthur Bridge, and watched the new Poplar St. Bridge being built, which eventually would be the Interstate carrier over the Mississippi River into St. Louis. Also the new Busch Stadium was being built in downtown St Louis, which would be home to the St. Louis Cardinals.

He was still training at Memphis TN one weekend per month and was a Crew Chief, and flew as Flight Engineer, Radar operator, MAD/Sonobuoy operator, and Bombardier positions in P2V Patrol Aircraft, and really enjoyed it. At liftoff speed, the pilot would call out, "Reaching rotation speed." The Flight Engineer would reply, "Two turning and all OK, Sir." A Navy transport would pick them up at St. Louis on Friday night, and return on Sunday evening. At this time he had a 1957 Chevrolet 2-dr hardtop.

On the weekend of December 20, 1959, George was Night flying against simulated Threat Emitters at NAS Memphis. It was late at night when he returned to the hangar, and he had a message to call home. It was very late, and he called back the next morning. Kathryn's Mother and Aunt had taken Kathryn to the Centerville hospital and their second son Gale Alvin was born. When he returned on Sunday evening, he went to the hospital, to visit their new son, and Kathryn. He took annual leave until Kathryn and Gale were ready to return home. Her mother stayed to care for them.

March 1960, He went on Active Duty for Training. They flew in P2Vs from the Naval Air Station [NAS] at Memphis, TN to NAS North Island, CA for operation against actual submarines, and on patrol flights. They stopped at NAS Dallas, TX for refueling, and saw a blood spot on the ramp. George inquired what had happened, and was told that a young Sailor had became hypnotized by a rotating propeller, and walked into it the night before. This was a warning that was stressed during basic Airman training. In other words, never look into a rotating propeller, because it would hypnotize you and natural instinct was to walk directly into it. The aircrew carried groceries on the airplanes, and had cooking facilities in the airplane for use during long patrol missions. These included steaks, baked potatoes, and either green beans or peas. On one flight 450 miles Southwest of San Diego, the right engine started to sputter. George was flying as Flight Engineer, so he adjusted the fuel mixture and other controls and got that engine operating smoothly. Just then the other engine was doing the same thing. Finally both engines were running smoothly. In any case the crew were wearing life jackets, and were prepared to "ditch". Then the pilot told the crew that their radio was out, and the IFF [Identification, Friend or Foe] was inoperative. Soon they had a fighter escort, guiding them to North Island to land. After security clearance they parked the P2V on the ramp. The entire crew went to temporary quarters, cleaned up, dressed in civilian clothes, and went to the city to have dinner and a couple of beers. They were discussing the airplane and engine trouble. They came up with the idea that they had idled for quite some time waiting for take-off at the end of the runway. The Commander asked what to do. George told him that if the carburetors were gummed up, he could run the engines to full power, and "shoot" the de-icing fluid [alcohol] to them. The Commander said, "Come on, let's try it."

They drove to the airplane in a rental car, in civilian clothes. The Commander climbed to the cockpit, and started the engines while another mechanic stood by with a fire bottle. The Commander ran the engines to full power, and pushed the de-icing button. The engines ran smoothly, the magneto check was perfect and the commander started the shutdown procedures.

Just when the aircraft was completely secured, the Security Officer came and arrested the crew, checked their ID, and took and took them to the Security Office. The Security Officer lectured them and since he knew they were reservists, asked what each man's profession was. The Lt. Commander said he was an attorney, specializing in Military Tribunals. The Security officer then released them and they went to their billets for the night.

The next day, George was flying as MAD/Sonobouy operator He would fly searching for a magnetic indication on the MAD [Magnetic Airborne Detector] Once he detected a magnetic source, he would immediately tell the pilot to initiate a circular pattern with the MAD pickup in the approximate center. He would then tell the Bombardier when to drop the Sonobuoys. He then monitored the sounds from the Sonobuoys, and pinpoint the location of the submarine. Once located, he would tell the pilot how to maneuver to the spot, and drop a PDC [Practice Depth Charge] where they though the submarine was. When one PDC exploded, the submarine commander said in the radio, "Damn, you dropped that direct on my conning tower". On one return to St Louis in a P2V on Sunday afternoon, the weather was rainy and foggy. The approach was on radar, and the pilot wasn't sure they were on the runway until they touched down, then they could see the runway.

Also in the first part of 1960, Kathryn's mother leased her land to David Claypool for oil exploration. He drilled the first well, which George was observing frequently, and during the finishing with a "spudder", The oil gushed out of the well, and shot up in the air about 65 feet and poured crude oil over everybody and everything. David ran in to shut the valve off, and it took him what seemed like an eternity to get it turned off. The valve had crude oil on it and David was covered in crude oil, but he had a smile on his face, signifying success. He finally got it shut off, and went over to discuss what had occurred. The Geologist agreed that they had penetrated a "Pimple gas pocket." After about 30 minutes it settled down, was diverted to the storage tank, and finally quit flowing, at which time a pump had to be installed for the well. A few days later on the weekend, George took Kathryn's mother, who had been keeping Dale while Kathryn worked, to her home in Flora. When they arrived, her phone was ringing. It was a reporter from the Chicago Sun-Times, wanting a story on the well. George told him that it wasn't worth a story, that he had been raised around the oil field, and it just was a gas pimple, and it soon ebbed, and was not out of the ordinary. The reporter printed a story on the front page of Sunday's paper. It was portraying George as the rich son-in-law, and guessing what he was going to do with the Millions he got from the oil well."

In August 1960, George was promoted to Equipment Specialist, GS-9, in The Directorate of Materiel. A friend, who George had worked for in his entry level in the Directorate of Engineering, was his supervisor. Again, George was the expert on the H-19 Helicopter, and advised supply specialists on part numbers, approximate weight, and size of components to determine shipping costs. He also developed schedules and budget for repair and overhaul of the H-19 Helicopter and components. Also, he would analyze resources and facilities for overhaul and modification, and program maintenance to insure orderly input to achieve maximum utilization of facilities and contract services.

He traveled to NAS Pensacola, FL, to meet with the personnel involved with the overhaul/rebuild of their engines. One of the Civilian employees was a retired Chief Petty Officer [CPO] that George had worked for when stationed at Ellyson Field in Pensacola. He immediately recognized George, and they had a joyous time reminiscing over their experiences during the day and after work that day.

George rented a larger 3-bedroom house .in front of the small house, which had only one bedroom, in which they had been residing. The owner of both houses moved to a new house, and this was the chance to get into a more livable house, which had more bedrooms He installed the Natural Gas system in both houses, and was still working as a Real Estate Broker. When checking the gas lines in the attic, he had a flashlight and a hammer in his hands. He slipped, and fell through the ceiling, in front of the sofa where Kathryn and Dale were sitting. They were as surprised as he was, and of course he had to repair the ceiling. As he was a Real Estate Broker he purchased lots in Belleville IL with the intention of building a house on them. He met with a contractor on designing and building a house with a basement on the lots, and also on constructing only a basement. He cleaned the lots off on weekends, and when he was about finished, the engine on the mower he was using fell apart, and threw a rod. He purchased another mower and finished cleaning the lot.

There was an advertisement for sealed bids on a house that was to be moved for the construction of Interstate 64. Also, the broker he worked with had the land near the intersection of U.S 159 and the new Interstate 64 listed for sale. There were no businesses around the new intersection at that time. George obtained bids on constructing a basement and moving the house to Belleville. His bid for the house was second highest, so he didn't get it.

Mr. Lehn, a friend at work who had moved from Corpus Christi, TX, needed a lot for location of his Mobile Home, which had been in a trailer park. George offered him one lot for a little more than he had paid for the two lots, and Mr. Lehn accepted. Later, Mr. Lehn bought the other lot for the same price he paid for the first one.

George resigned in May, 1962 due to the lack of promotion possibilities, withdrew his retirement fund, and purchased a 60 acre farm northwest of Xenia. He sold the 2 houses at 1853 Doris Ave for the owner. They moved to Flora, IL to a house near the High School and Washington grade school, while they were remodeling the farmhouse.

That summer his Grandmother passed away in San Bernardino, CA where his aunt, Eva, the only sister of his father, resided and had a Real Estate office. She was shipped to St. Louis, MO., where the Undertaker, Newton J. Branson of Flora picked her up. The funeral was held at the Funeral Home, with burial at Xenia. Afterward, all the family gathered for refreshments at their house.

It was here that they bought their first new upright freezer They purchased it from Montgomery Ward for $88.00.It was finally scrapped in 1997, during the move from Dothan to Greenville, AL.

That fall, Dale started school at Washington School, about two blocks from their house, in the first grade. When he came home in the evening, the first thing he done was locate the daily newspaper and read it. One day, the teacher was throwing basketballs to the students during recess. He was after one ball, and another grabbed Dale to take the ball. Dale objected and ripped the other boy's shirt in the scuffle. The boy's mother called Kathryn to tell her that Dale had torn her boy's shirt. Kathryn asked George what we should do, and he told her to buy the boy a new shirt. This was a common occurrence at school, and he thought there was no use of making an issue of it. That summer, they farmed, and remodeled the country house they had bought. They had a water well drilled, installed an automatic electric pump and hot water heater, bought new kitchen cabinets, leveled the front of the house and poured a concrete porch, paneled the walls in the living room, installed new flooring in the living room, kitchen and bath. They installed hot and cold-water connections on the enclosed back porch for washer hookups, and re-roofed the part over the living room, kitchen, and bath.

They moved into farmhouse the fall of 1953, and Dale started school at Xenia, riding the school bus every day. The teacher told George and Kathryn that Dale seemed to be bored with classroom work. She recommended that he start music lessons to occupy his time. George and Kathryn agreed, and he started music lessons. On the farm they installed electric fences, and had hogs and cattle, as well as planting and harvesting grain. They also had a garden and canned vegetables, jelly, and fruits, mainly peaches. They worked hard that summer, as well as starting a Cub Scout Pack, and Kathryn was a den mother. Dale was a cub scout, and the scouts had several projects.

George was applying Nitrogen to corn with an Anhydrous Ammonia applicator. He was using what was called a "Nurse tank" to fill the applicator. While filling the applicator from the nurse tank, a high pressure hose about 2 inches in diameter busted and spread anhydrous everywhere, including George. Anyone who has used that material knows that when the ammonia hits air, it is extremely cold and suffocating. When the hose busted, George was overtaken with the Ammonia and breathing stopped for one to two minutes before he could get the valve on the nurse tank shut off. This affected him for two to three days afterward.

When President Kennedy was assassinated, Kathryn was in Flora at the laundry, and George was at home. The news came over the CB [Citizens Band] radio before the news media got the story. The CB was the only base to mobile communication they had, and it was used quite frequently.

On May 23, 1963, George's mother got a call from Russellville Arkansas that his grandmother Smith had passed away from cancer. She was transported to Flora, where her funeral was conducted. Since George's grandfather's death, she had stayed at her home in Flora, and frequently visited her two daughters at Xenia and Russellville, Arkansas.

The winter of 1963, George worked as a welder on the night shift at Valley Steel Co. in Flora.

In 1964 he, and his father traveled to Hayti, Missouri and bought two self-propelled combines; a John Deere 55 14 ft and an International 141 12 ft with a two row corn head. The International 12 ft header was loaded on their truck. George and a cousin, Gene Lane drove the combines to Xenia, IL. Ground speed was about 8 miles per hour. This took two days, and they went through 3 drive belts on the International. It took over one hour to go up a long hill on I-57. Also, when they crossed the Mississippi River Bridge between Missouri to Illinois, it was difficult to stop traffic until they were clear. The International had a two-row corn head on it and the John Deere that George was driving had the 14 ft. grain header on it. As mentioned before, they had the 12 ft. grain header on the truck for the International. George later traded the International for a new 1964 Chevrolet, at St. Peter, IL where the Chevrolet dealer was also an International farm equipment dealer.

In 1964 George was appointed a County Deputy Sheriff. One of the main events other than patrolling and assistance occurred one Saturday. A teenager that worked for him wanted to get off at noon, because his mother told him that they had some friends coming to visit. About an hour after noon, the Sheriff pulled up to his house and said, "Get in, George, We have a problem." He got in the cruiser with the Sheriff and sped off. George did not know then that they were headed for the home of the teenager that had worked for him that morning. When they got there, the Undertaker was there, as well as several onlookers. The Sheriff told George on the way that they had a suicide. The teen's mother had gotten his shotgun and one shell, went to the barn loft, and evidently lay on a blanket, covered up with another blanket, and shot herself in the chest by pulling the trigger with her toe. No one ever knew what the reason was. The Sheriff and George assisted the undertaker to get her out of the barn loft and into the hearse, and prepare a report of the incident.

About the same time, there were forest fires in the area, either caused by lightening or carelessness on the part of hunters and hikers. George and others used the CB radios to communicate between each other and to the fire fighters. They would drive to the fires through lanes, and re-lay the location and intensity of the fire to the fire fighters. The CB was the main method of communication then, and CB clubs were organized everywhere. They could talk to anyone in the US by relay through base stations. All truck drivers had them and they were used for emergency communication and chitchat. CB sales and repair flourished. They had an assigned frequency assigned and their individual call letters. Sometimes, they could talk to operators as far away as California. This was a character-istic of weather, called "Skip" that allowed them to communicate that far. The normal range was about 10 miles on mobile and about 25 miles with a base unit. The base unit distance was dependant on the antenna system the operator was using.

During this time George got interested in crude oil exploration and production. He collected and studied geological reports and maps, and be-came adept at reading Electric Logs of wells drilled. He could then project future production possibilities and trends from the wells that were previously drilled. His childhood cousin and friend Don was an Independent Operator, which meant he drilled the wells, finished them, and produced them, without being connected with any Oil Company. He obtained his investors to cover the cost of drilling and producing.

He also researched, studied and became adept radio and TV repair and service.

In the early winter George was called by a neighbor who ran an oil well service business, to assemble a truck engine a former employee had disassembled and left. He spent two days in assembling the engine and installing it in the truck. When it came time to time the engine, the manager said, "George, you have done enough. Let's take it downtown to get it timed." So, they towed the truck to the garage. It was cold, and they had to wear heavy coats. Also, George drove a water truck for him for a couple of weeks, delivering water to customers loading and delivering salt water for disposal.

Later, George obtained a position at Stanford Engineering in Salem in their sales department, handling orders and inquiries for paper cutting machines.

In January 1965, George received a call from St. Louis, that they wanted him back at USAAVSCOM [U.S Army Aviation Systems Command] to fill a position as GS-9, at $7465 per year, in the Directorate of Maintenance. They wanted him to start immediately.

The job included performing Maintenance Engineering analysis of data; evaluate performance of equipment to determine requirements for modification; and revision of work specifications. Develop techniques for analysis of data, and develop computer programs. His principal task was to implement and manage The Army Equipment Records System [TAERS] for Army aircraft, which was the Log Book for the aircraft, and the various forms for Time Change and Retirement components. For example rotor blades were retirement time items. If the records were lost, it was mandatory to scrap the blade, even if it appeared to be or was new. He located, traced and reconstituted records on those items, saving the cost of scrapping or re-overhaul. He rented a house in Belleville, IL for a few months where Dale went to school. It was winter when they moved, and snow was thick. He borrowed his father's truck for the move. He was not happy with the house in Belleville because he had a camera stolen from his auto, and they found where someone had entered the house through a window. In the summer he found a house in Mascoutah, IL, through a fellow worker. It was at 440 South Railway Ave, and had a large garden in the rear. It was next door to the school principal. The neighbor, Mr. Highland had boys in the same age range of Dale. Although Gale was not 6 years old until December, it was decided to enter him in the First Grade at Mascoutah. George carpooled with three others who lived in the Mascoutah area. One lived across the street from him.

Just after George began working, a lady approached him and told George that she had married Bill, George's former supervisor, and he was trying to borrow money to buy liquor from friends. George replied, "No, I wouldn't loan him a cent for that purpose, but I would buy him a steak dinner anywhere he desired." She then asked George to visit him in his hotel room, and try to persuade him to change his lifestyle. George asked "why me?" She replied, "because he thought a lot of you and was very upset when you resigned from the Directorate of Materiel. He highly respects you, and if he will listen to you, he might change his outlook." George visited Bill in his hotel room, and tried to persuade him to have dinner at a local restaurant. Bill would not listen to George, and it appeared he was surviving on liquor and cigarettes. He was found dead in the hotel room some time later.

Mascoutah was a typical German community, and each morning small children would go to the tavern and get their grandfather a bucket of beer for the day.

During this time George was named Assistant District Director [ADD] for the Boy Scouts of America, in Belleville, IL. He attended several meetings at Scott Air Force Base and initially had 8 Scout Troops and Cub Scout dens to assist. He visited those units and assisted them in any way possible. Another District Director was a retired Air Force Warrant Officer, which became good friends with George. One ADD resigned, and George was assigned 8 additional units to assist. He was visiting a unit every night of the week, sometimes two on one night. Job pressures were getting greater, travel was increasing and George told the District Director that he had to phase back or resign as ADD. The Director told George, "I hate to hear that, but you have to put your family and your job first. We have trouble obtaining capable ADD, and I consider you one of the best. I have had nothing but the best comments from all your units." George wrote the DD a letter of resignation. After he resigned, some of the units called George and thanked him for his assistance. Another ADD was in a meeting at Scott Air Force Base one Saturday, and said that his wife was getting angry at his activities with the Scouts She asked him, "What am I going to tell the policeman when our son gets in trouble. Should I tell him that his father is at a Scout meeting?" He said he replied, "Yes, tell him the truth, but remember that hasn't happened yet."

George attended several computer courses sponsored by at IBM in St Louis between February and May1965. The Army had a massive IBM 360 computer system in the building that encompassed one entire floor. They had hundreds of Key Punch operators throughout the building, that all they did was to operate Key Punch Machines. All input was controlled by punched cards, and they had several Programmers that wrote programs for processing data. Many other employees were taught basic programming techniques, processing techniques, etc. This IBM system cost approximately eight million dollars.

It was about this time that George was selected to be a member of the Red Ball Express group. This was a group of experts from maintenance, supply and procurement that worked 12 hours per day for 7days, then went back to their directorate for a week to work the normal 8 hour schedule. This alternating continued for three months. The group expedited repair parts to the U.S troops in Viet Nam. George made many friends art all the Army Depots and Contractor facilities, where he would locate items in critical supply, and turn them over to the Supply representative of the Contract Representative for expedited shipment. On one occasion George located an engine at an Army Depot, which overhauled them. He found one, and had it shipped. The Director of Supply called George into his office and asked him where he found that engine. George replied, "The only place in this world it existed." The supply Director replied, "This printout says we don't have any serviceable engines anywhere." George said, while reading his printout upside down, "That is what we are here 12 hours per day; to bypass the slow computer." The director replied, "I don't like that, but I guess I can't do anything about it." George replied, "Yes, Sir, you have summed it up about right." George filled about 75 percent of the red ball requisitions for EDP [Equipment Deadlined for Parts] in Viet Nam.

On another occasion, on Sunday, George obtained the manufacturer name of a fuel tank for the UH-1 from a friend at the Corpus Christi Army Depot. George located the manufacturer, and the Company President answered. George said, Good after noon, Sir. Would you happen to have any fuel tanks available on Contract with the Army?" The President answered, "Yes, I just happen to have four that just came out of production yesterday. When do you need them, yesterday?" George said, "Just a minute, I'll turn you over to the procurement representative to arrange shipment." The procurement representative arranged to get the tanks packed that day and air shipped that night to Travis Air Force Base for forwarding to Viet Nam.

In February 1966, he was promoted to GS-11, at $8961 per year. Here he had about the same duties as before, but was a member of the Data Requirements Review Board and assistant Chief of the Configuration Management Branch of the Directorate of Maintenance. One day in 1966, George was on U.S 460 at the entrance to the Shrine of The Lady of The Snows, when a car in front of him attempted a U-turn in front of him. He tried to evade him, but the accident crashed the entire left side of his 1964 Chevrolet. He was lucky to only have broken glass all over him and in his pants cuffs. He managed to pull onto the shoulder, near a large drop-off and called on the CB radio for someone to call his house, and call a wrecker in Mascoutah to tow him in. Since he had to have transportation, he traded the Chevrolet for a new 1966 Oldsmobile Delta 88, with the understanding that he would get the Chevrolet repaired. Also he had a 1964 Volkswagen about this time, that he drove to work until it blew an engine on the McArthur Bridge, and he had to be pushed on to the St. Louis side. He called a shop in Belleville, IL, had it towed in and traded it later for a 1966 Ford Mustang.

It was this time that he decided to make a career of Federal Service. He re-deposited his retirement funds that he had previously withdrawn when he resigned before. He was determined to continue his education, and placed his attention to get better qualified and sometime to retire with a decent living.

From January through March, George attended the Army Logistics Management course at The U.S. Army Logistics Management Center at Ft. Lee, VA. He traveled with a co-worker, John Mazar and shared a room with him. The room had two twin beds and they shared the bathroom. This was a 12-week course, the longest offered at Ft. Lee. This was considered the equivalent of a Master's Degree, and it was just after this that George was invited to be a member of the Society of Logistics Engineers [SLE]. At Ft Lee, there were several foreign Military students, ranking from Captain to Colonel. On weekends they visited several Civil War sites and one weekend they visited Williamsburg, Virginia. As a project, George was assigned the Defense Attorney for a mock trial of a middle manager who was threatened for extinction. Another project was management of a contract for production of Defense Materiel. The contract was let to two companies, and all kinds of problems erupted in both plants. The class was divided into work groups, and each group had to program corrective actions and insert them into the computer. In the final portion, one plant burned completely and the production in the other plant had to be doubled to make up the difference. Then the problem was whether to locate another contractor or to continue with the one that survived. During these three months he had to send the term paper for Kathryn to type. During this time Kathryn had fallen through a weak board in the floor near the rear door, and a neighbor had to help her out of it. He returned home early in the morning after driving all night, and Kathryn's mother and Dale had the mumps. The graduation paper is at Appendix A. It was about this time that George was visiting his father who then lived in Flora, IL, when he called George aside and said, "Guess what? I someone tried to poison me with arsenic." He named the person, but George was sworn not to relate that person to anyone. George replied, "I can't hardly believe that. What made you sure it was that person?" He then told George about feeling ill and going to the Doctor. The person made some comment to his father, indicating that he deserved it. George asked, "Why did they think you deserved that?" His father replied, " Nothing, she said it was on general principles." He told them that he had the event well documented and if it ever occurred again they would be charged with murder. George's father said, " If I should die from that cause, you know the Doctor, and he has all the documentation. You know what to do in that event." He couldn't do anything about it because of family considerations, but was alert for any more threats.

George took a boat home to Mascoutah that his father had bought which needed some repair. He spent much of the spring completely recovering the exterior with fiberglass, painting it, refinishing the interior, and replaced the cushions. They took it to Omega Lake that summer, and really enjoyed it.

It was during this time the Arch on the Riverfront was under construction, and George was privileged to watch the entire process to completion. He watched the last section of the Arch be installed from the upper floor of the Mart Building.

In November 1967, he was promoted to GS-12, in the Logistics Management Division, Project Manager, UTTAS [Utility Tactical Transport Aircraft System] that would be later the UH-60 Blackhawk. It was then in Concept Formulation stage, when it was not known whether it would be a Rotary or Fixed wing aircraft. The Deputy Project Manager was an Aerospace Engineer, Conrad Busse, who George had known for some time, and had developed a good working relationship. George developed the Maintenance Support Plan, the earliest of the life cycle ever, and assisted in development of the Integrated Logistics Support Plan, the first new system it was to be applied to. He was assigned to working groups in trade-off studies and those concerned with the design evaluation and recommendations. It was here that Mr. Busse and LTC "Deke" Descouteau [sp] sat down at his desk and told him that he had about two years of College, and it was time for him to either complete it of forget about it. They told him to work out some way to complete his degree in Aerospace Engineering, and they would support him all the way. George called a Professor at Parks College,

Tom Harrington who he had known well during his past attendance at Parks. His plan called for him to take two or three classes in succession each day, and make up the time at work, on Tuesday and Thursday evenings and Saturdays, or in other words change his working hours. Mr.Busse, the Personnel Director and the Commanding General approved it. George worked two evenings and Saturday each week and continued until December 1969, when he received his BS degree in Aircraft Maintenance Engineering, and FAA Aircraft and Power plant Certificate. He stated that for two years all he did was work, go to school, study, eat and sleep.

In 1968, they started to look for a house located so George wouldn't have to travel through East St. Louis, because of the increase in trouble there, and in Madison County due to lower taxes. On one trip a carpool of females headed home from work on their way to Mascoutah and had shots fired in the trunk of their car. They sped away, and found another route to travel. Another airport manager from central Illinois was going through East St Louis on the same route at night with his convertible top down, and a rock was thrown and shattered his windshield.

They bought their first new house at 41 Orchid Dr, on the corner of Orchid Drive and Pat Drive, north of Collinsville, with 3 bedrooms and an attached garage. George bought and installed the air conditioner in the house. When connecting the electrical lead, he was easing the wire into the appropriate slot. Suddenly the needle-nosed pliers slipped and the next thing he knew he was laying on the floor of the basement. When the pliers slipped, he hit the line voltage and was knocked out for a while. Needless to say, he called an electrician to complete the task.

During this time, George attended the Research and Development course, and the Army Project Manager courses at Ft Lee, VA.

In January 1969, he was promoted to GS-13 due to ob re-evaluation, at $14,409.00 per year.

George was working one Saturday on the 10th floor of the Mart building, as a result of changing working hours to attend college in pursuit of an Engineering degree. The power went out in his office, so he moved to the conference room near a window. He had a battery-powered radio, so he turned it on to find what was happening. He found that all radio stations were off the air. He had all the office work he was reviewing, when the building started to shake. He grabbed everything he had in the conference room, put it on his desk, and went to the interior of the building. The shaking was so severe he thought that the building would crumble. He called home, and asked Kathryn what was happening there. She related that they had an earthquake, and the house shook too, about 20 miles away from the office.

In 1969, he traded for a new Ford in Collinsville.

In November 1969, he was detailed to GS-13 for the Project Manager for Utility Aircraft. This was interesting, because he was the supervisor for Grant Aid and Foreign Military Sales, for 38 countries, and Chinese and German Co- Production programs for the UH-1 and T-53 engines. He sold 50 twin-engine versions of the UH-1 to Canada. The Canadians made several visits to St Louis to finalize the purchase of the UH-1N [Twin engine version of the UH-1D]. It was a real pleasure to meet and talk to the Canadian Air Force Officers. During this time George had the pleasure of traveling to Germany to brief the German Air Force on how the US supported the UH-1D in their Army. George prepared the briefing and planned the entire trip for himself, Col. Lauderbach from St Louis and Chuck Rapp from the Corpus Christi Army Depot. Their wives had been invited to accompany them, but if one would not go, none would go. Kathryn was afraid to fly overseas, and another wife had conflicts, so none of the wives accompanied them. They all flew frequently on TWA, and were members of the Ambassador's Club. This helped to endure the long layovers at Airports.

They left from St. Louis, flew to New York, and left for London, England from Kennedy Airport. They flew what seemed like all night, and arrived in London just after daybreak. A group of Chinese businessmen were checking out of their hotel, so they went to a nearby Café for lunch while their rooms were cleaned. They checked in to the hotel right after noon, and then toured London that afternoon and the next morning. They rode on the double-decker busses, saw the Changing of The Guard at the Queens Palace, toured Westminster Abbey, saw bomb damage from World II, saw the Big Ben clock, the Queen and Prince Charles driving to a smaller church near the Palace, and many other sights of London. In the afternoon, they boarded the airplane to Bonn, Germany. At the check-in for the flight, the agent told the Colonel that he had excessive baggage, and he would have to pay an additional twelve dollars. The reason for the excessive baggage was briefing material to be presented to the German Air Force. The Colonel became enraged, and said, "Dammit, George, I left it up to you to arrange this trip, and now you have screwed it up." George replied, " I will pay the damn difference, and you can go on to Germany without me, because I am going back to St. Louis." He then cooled off, and he said, "George, you did an outstanding job arranging this trip and preparing the briefing. You are the expert on this type of work, and I need you to go on with us." The Colonel paid the additional fee and never mentioned it again. When they arrived in Bonn, an escort, an Army Captain from the American Embassy met and greeted them, and took them to the hotel downtown, near the train station in Munich. The hotel was much different than what they were accustomed to. The toilet tank was mounted on the wall about 5 feet above the bowl. It was cold, and they asked the desk for some blankets. Desk clerk laughed, and told them that in Europe, the "Feather bed" was to cover up with, not to lie on.

The next day the escort took them to the Headquarters, Federal Republic of Germany where a robust German General greeted them. The first thing the General did after the introductions was to offer each of them a cigar to smoke with him. After an informal chat, and smoking cigars, he called his Senior Staff in, introduced the visitors, and they sat down for the briefing on how the USA supported their UH-1D and T-53 engines in the U.S. Army. Afterwards, they had an informal discussion with Coffee, and were thanked by all of the Federal Republic of Germany [FRG] officers. The next morning they left to go to the T-53 Engine factory for a tour of the facility. All the German employees were very friendly and courteous. An engine coming off the production was weighed, and came to within 3 grams of the Specification weight. All workers clapped and had smiles on their faces, because they were proud to have a part in the production. The pride in workmanship was evident.

The next day, they journeyed to the to the UH-1D factory. On the route, they passed through a small town and saw the German women sweeping the street. At the plant, they discovered that the airframe parts were hand made, and spare parts were not pre-drilled, because all drilling patterns were different. Therefore, each airframe part had to be fabricated for the designated UH-1D. The quality was better than the USA, and they took more pride in manufacturing. The panels were sent to field units without being pre-drilled. The field unit had to find the drill pattern and drill and rivet the replacement panels. Each UH-1D had its own drawings versus one set for each UH-1D series helicopters in the USA. Their inspection intervals were different, and levels of maintenance were different, but they had a lower failure rate, and better availability rate than the USA.

The Plant Manager and his senior staff treated them to lunch. The lunch lasted for about three hours, with 14 Courses. The Colonel got a sickly feeling about half way through the lunch, and the Plant Manager went to the front of the restaurant, and brought back a small bottle of liquid, and told the Colonel to drink it. The Colonel hesitated awhile, and asked what was in it. The manager told him it was a herbal remedy for all stomach ailments. The Colonel drank it, and felt better in a few minutes, and they finished their lunch. They then returned to the hotel to freshen up for Dinner with the factory executives. At the dinner, when they arrived at the restaurant, the Plant Manager's secretary was in the group and spoke English fluently. As a social courtesy, George helped her remove her coat, and a German lady uttered a comment. He asked her what she said, and she told him that she said, "He is spoiling that lady." The Secretary said that she had a sister married to an American Air Force Officer stationed in Montgomery, AL. She remarked that the Europeans valued the American citizenship more than most Americans. Their escort took them back to the hotel, where they slept well under their feather beds.

The next day, they took the train South to Lengrese and Bad Toltz, where the Colonel had been stationed when he was an Army Captain. They visited the lady that tended his daughter when he was stationed there, who lived just outside of town in a barn on the lower level as customary in Germany. When she saw the Colonel, she gave him a big hug, and tears came from her, because she was afraid he would never return, and congratulated him on his success. Her son worked on the ski slopes, and she had just made a Cherry pie. She insisted they have a slice of pie and coffee with her as a celebration. She also had a daughter who worked at a restaurant in town and wished the visitors could meet her children. On their way back to town, they stopped at a bar near the train station. The owner remembered the Colonel, and insisted on them having a free beer. The beer in

Germany is served warm [not cooled] from a tap. The Germans will spend all day playing cards and sipping beer, and never get drunk. He said that an American would gulp the beer down, and in two hours be thrown out as drunk and disorderly. It was interesting that the train was full of skiers with their skis on the way down, and many were injured on the way back to Munich. The trains were all exactly on time, with no delays.

After their return trip, they freshened up in their hotel. They then went to a small restaurant near the hotel. Their were only two other customers, and the waiter did not speak English. They motioned that they wanted fish, and finally he understood. He left for what seemed like an eternity, and came in with a bucket of water with 3 live Trout in it. He shook his head as if that was okay. They motioned for him to cook them up for them. When the fish came out, they were served with a baked potato, and all the "Brochins" (hard, round rolls) they wanted. The fish were fried with the heads and fins on and were really delicious.

The next day, they checked out of the hotel after breakfast, and were taken to the Airport. They boarded a Boeing 707, with a stopover in Brussels, Belgium. At Brussels, they were scheduled for a one-hour layover, but it turned out to be three hours. The Belgium people were very cold and rude compared to the Germans, and seemed to delay us as long as possible. The Terminal had a large liquor store, and the store was very busy, because travelers wanted to buy their liquor because of was much cheaper cost than anywhere else, and they had a captive audience. When they took off from Brussels, the 707 had been heavily loaded with fuel for the direct flight to New York. They used almost all the runway for take-off. Since they were five hours ahead of New York time, they arrived in New York three hours later, New York time. When they returned to St. Louis, it took a full week to adjust to the time difference.

In July 1970, George was reassigned as a Product Assurance Specialist in the office of the Project Manager for the Manned Aerial Surveillance and Target Acquisition System [MASTS]. This was the OV-1D, which was in Limited Production, undergoing testing and evaluation. The testing had floundered for four years, and didn't seem to be culminating. This was because the Project Manager had no one he considered having the experience and knowledge to manage it. This was the most complex system ever tested by the Army. It had approximately 180 deficiencies [serious problems] and 300 shortcomings. George was assigned the task of getting all the deficiencies, and most of the shortcomings corrected, and assist in getting it type classified as Standard. It was an electronic nightmare. The Project Manager was Col. John Love, who was a top notch Colonel. Col Love told George that he had the full responsibility and all the resources he needed to accomplish the task George worked hand in hand with the Director of the Engineering Division, Dale Hamilton, an elderly engineer, who had experienced health problems, but was very sharp and excellent to work with. This is where George learned electronics very well. He traveled to all the test activities, the Pentagon, the Army Materiel Command in Washington DC, the Test and Evaluation Command in Aberdeen, MD, and several Contractors and Laboratories, to obtain what had to be accomplished to correct the problems and Type Classification completed. George, and Dale Hamilton called monthly meetings with all participants, and made notes on all Deficiencies and Shortcomings on what had to be done to eliminate them as well as who was responsible. They called these meetings in St Louis in the summer to resolve these problems. They found that in the winter, they had trouble with attendance in St. Louis so they called the winter meetings at Ft Huachuca, Arizona and had a packed house every month. The Arizona State Troopers were happy to have the attendees, because they issued several speeding tickets when traveling to and from the airport at Tucson, AZ.

In December 1969, George received his B.S. Degree in Aircraft Maintenance Engineering from Parks College of St. Louis University, at Cahokia, IL. Kathryn and both sons attended the graduation with him.

In 1971, he traded his older Ford Pickup for a new Ford F-250 pickup. He could haul 6000 lbs of grain on the farm. It would get 10 miles per gallon, whether it was empty or loaded. It had all the accessories on it, including automatic transmission, and a 351 engine. The family had been traveling to the farm almost every weekend, where Dale began driving tractors.

In July 1971 George was assigned as a Supervisory General Engineer, at the same grade. Col. Love assigned two technicians to him and told him that he had proven the capability to perform not only Aerospace Engineering, but also Electronic and Electrical Engineering duties. By April 1972, he had corrected most of the problems solved. The two technicians took reassignments and his job was changed to Product Assurance Engineer. It was here that he was referred to as "Big George" for the way he got actions taken care of.

He had been working on a MA in International Relations at the University Of Oklahoma, spent two weeks in a Seminar at the University. He wrote a Thesis, titled, "The Probable Effect of The Chinese Proletarian Cultural Revolution on Government Structure as Represented By The Peking Foreign Language Press" [attached as Appendix B}. He then started a MA degree in Business with Webster University, and the classes were conducted at the same building that he worked in after duty hours. Classes were held after working hours, so no duty time was expended. Seventeen Semester hours were transferred from the University of Oklahoma MLS program to the Webster University MBA program.

Back at work, the Project Office prepared the Type Classification Package, with all the Project Manager Division divisions. George was designated to hand carry the package to Washington, DC to the Pentagon and Army Materiel Command [AMC] Headquarters for approval. He took an early flight to DC, and walked the package to all who had approval authority, and ended up at the AMC [Army Materiel Command] Headquarters, which was near the National Airport. About 4:00 PM he had all the approvals except one. The last approval had to be obtained from a senior civilian who was in a meeting. About 4:30 PM Washington time, he had the last signature He called Col Love, and told him he had all the approvals and to have someone available to put the package in the safe, because it was classified as Secret. Col Love told him not to get too anxious, that the nearby motel was not bad at all. George replied, that within an hour he would be on his way back to St. Louis. As soon as George got off the telephone, he thanked the personnel he had been meeting with and headed for the Airport. He obtained a flight for St. Louis in about 30 minutes.

He arrived in St. Louis about 6:30 that evening, and called the office. Col Love answered the phone, and asked where he was. George told him he was in St. Louis, and would be at the office in about 40 minutes. When George got to the office, Col Love was waiting. George asked him why someone else did not stay, and he told him, "I wouldn't miss this opportunity for anything." He locked the package in the safe, locked the office, ant told George, "Lets stop by the Officer's Club and have a drink. You deserve it." When they left the Club, he told George to take the next day off, that he had accomplished three days work in one day.

Also, George was on a Global Positioning System [GPS] Tri-Service working group, because the OV-1D had an Inertial Navigation System, for which the GPS would provide the next generation of navigation systems.

They were overjoyed when the first GPS Satellite was launched. There were to be eight satellites before the system was functional for Military use.

The next Monday COL Love called all the Division Chiefs, [George was director of the Product Assurance and Test Division], and told them that their job as Project Manager was finished. All would be reassigned to other positions by the end of the month. The Colonel tasked one of the Divisions to plan a party, since that would be the last time they would all be together. The day of the party, George had starter problems with his 1969 Ford when he left the parking lot in St. Louis. He stopped and bought a new starter on the way home. When he got home, he changed into coveralls, and changed the starter. Afterward, he showered and cleaned up, dressed in a suit, and went to the party near Lambert Field, on the western side of St. Louis. This was in December 1972.

George was reassigned to the Project Manager for Aircraft Survivability Equipment, in December 1972, as Chief of the Product Assurance and Test Division. His main job was to implement Reliability and Maintainability programs, and to manage the Test and Evaluation programs for advanced countermeasures to be installed on Army Aircraft. When he arrived at the PM-ASE, he was given a "Survival Kit" with a helmet, aspirin, Rolaids, Kleenex, and several similar items. Most of the projects were advanced technology, fast response, consisting of countermeasures to threat missiles and other threats, including Infrared, Radar, optical, Laser, etc., for all Army aircraft. Here he innovated combined Development and Operational testing. All equipment was badly need by the troops, and was classified as quick response, so some Contractors, Army Laboratories, and others worked diligently to meet the challenge. The normal time from development to fielding of a system was about 10 years, and they shortened this for most items to two years. They worked with the CIA and FBI to keep updated on current threats. This was a continuation of George's experience with the MASTS [OV-1] Project Manager, where he had a Top Secret security clearance with special access. This required him to read the intelligence reports weekly to keep up to date on world technological developments, and he had been trained on how to protect and preserve Security information. He served on working groups to evaluate Advanced Development progress and apply that technology to current needs.

Here, he had outstanding subordinates, who were dependable, cooperative, and reliable. Among these were his assistant Jerry Dettmer, Debbie Tregoning his Secretary, and his Reliability, Availability, and Maintainability expert, John Shannon. The Chief Engineer, Herb Murch was Chief of the Research and Development Division, was a top manager, and they worked close together on all projects. The Chief of the Program Management Division was a black lady, Thyra Bonds, who was an expert in her field, and became one of George's best friends. He was the first within the Department of Army to integrate Development and Operational testing, and coordinate tests during Advanced Development stage to eliminate all duplication and greatly reduce testing costs. There were approximately 55 to 60 tests going on at any time, which George kept up to date on all tests, and knew the status on all at any time. He was also a member of the ASE Permanent Steering Group to integrate Developer and User requirements in all current and proposed projects. George was instrumental in implementing the Operational Testing concept.

The Project Managers were COL Stewart Shirey and later COL Jack Keaton, who were both top-notch Army Colonels and were highly respected worldwide. George was also a member of the Officer's Club in the building. He would frequently stop with COL Shirey or Col. Keaton and many other friends for a drink before going home. Some one asked Col Keaton how long it took him to get home, and he would reply, "Two

Beers". He would order two unopened beers and leave. No one ever got stopped for DWI, DUI, nor had any accident on his way home.

George continued the Master of Business degree with Webster University in St. Louis.

This job required frequent travel, because of the Security classification. Most of the discussions had to be in a classified area, and secure phones were restricted for emergency communications only. Most trips by this office required the traveler to carry classified material, properly packaged. George traveled to a Contractor facility for a progress meeting in Nashua, New Hampshire, where the Program Manager there met him at the door, and told him they had some serious problems. George asked him for the list of problems, a phone and a Secretary for about 30 to 45 minutes. He agreed, and George gave the Secretary a list of phone numbers. She told him that after she got the first one, she would have the next one available when he finished the first one and so forth. This occurred for about 8 calls, and when he got off from a call, she would have the next one on line. George made notes, and finished the last call after about 35 minutes. He went to the Program Manager's office, briefed him, and told him the problems were solved. The Program Manager told George that that he knew of no one else that had the ability to do this, and if he ever needed another job, he had one there.

He attended several meetings with Grumman, the OV-1D Manufacturer, and made good friends with all the management. One was the Chief Engineer, who was German born, and they had several discussions about the OV-1D Mohawk, especially the rare occurrence when it would suddenly roll over upside down for no apparent reason. He had been searching for the cause, but had not found it. George suggested that it might be an electromagnetic interference in or with the autopilot. He thanked him for the idea, and said he had not thought of that aspect. He had been looking at the autopilot malfunctions only. They were friends and had many discussions over the next several years on this subject. To his knowledge this problem was never solved. The Mohawk years past had been nicknamed "The Widow Maker", because of the low survivable rate in crashes. The Army averaged losing three aircraft per year, whether in combat or not.

George had several meetings in the Southwest and West including Edwards Air Force Base CA, China Lake, CA, White Sands Missile Range, NM, Fort Bliss, TX, Contractor facilities at Scottsdale, AZ, and Fort Worth, TX. Also a contractor at West Palm Beach, FL, and Army Laboratories at Fort Monmouth, NJ, The Pentagon in Washington, DC, Ft Sill, OK, Fort Rucker, AL, Ft. Monroe, VA, Ft. Hood, TX, Ft Gordon, GA and others. He was known as a professional and an expeditor, by everyone he encountered. This was a massive coordination effort, due to the many laboratories, contractors, test activities, security agencies, Research and Development activities and other Department of Defense agencies that were involved.

At one meeting at Ft. Bliss, TX several attendees went to the Officer's Club bar for a few drinks and discussion. An Army LTC was sitting next to George, and the discussion came to where they were from. He asked George, and George told him a small town in the Midwest that he probably never heard of. George asked him where he was from, and he replied that he was from a small town in the Midwest that George probably never heard of. Both narrowed it down to Southern Illinois. He told George to mane it. George replied, "Xenia Illinois." He jumped up and yelled, "You are kidding. That's where my Grandfather lived when I stayed with him. I knew Kathryn, the Smith girls and several girls and boys that I can't recall their names now". George told him that he married Kathryn and the Smith girls were his cousins. They found that his grandfather lived across the street from Kathryn's house, and that he and Kathryn had played in the street together when they were young.

This job was very challenging, because as mentioned before, it involved Infrared, Radar, Optical, and Laser countermeasures on all Army aircraft. He also had meetings with the Navy, Air Force, and Marine personnel to exchange development activities on all countermeasures and protective devices. Of course, he had to keep up with the threat technology and apply that to the countermeasures.

During this time George and others organized the Southern Illinois Citizens League in opposition to the St. Louis, MO City Earnings Tax on Illinois residents who worked in St. Louis. In the Hearing, the St. Louis attorney said they knew it was wrong, but the City had to have the money to operate. The plea was denied in the Court.

Back at home George and Kathryn had left Gale while they ran some errands. When they returned, Gale was laying on the patio with two neighbor girls over him, cleaning him up. He had rode his bicycle down the hill in the front yard, the front wheel came off, and Gale had landed on the side of the street. The girls had seen the event, and helped Gale to the patio.

George researched janitorial supplies, cleaning solutions and disinfecting solutions, and started Belle Valley Chemical Co. He still was busy at his job, so he hired a salesman to sell these to hotels, schools, factories, etc. He mixed the solutions, and purchased the brushes, brooms, etc from the manufacturers, and had good reports from customers. His salesman needed his auto cleaned out, so he stored it in a washhouse at his father's home. One night the washhouse burned, destroying all the sales documentation, and supplies that George had provided to the salesman. After the fire, George decided to terminate the business, because he couldn't or didn't have the time to reassemble the supplies, and was unable to obtain another capable salesman.

He traded the Mustang for a new Mercury Capri. He still had the 1969 Ford LTD, which he had bought new. Inside the house, he installed shelving on the end of the counter surrounding the stairs leading to the basement. He also finished the basement for an office area, and a recreation room/lounge area.

During this time the family took vacations to Theodosia Lake, MO two years in a row, where they camped, fished and water-skied. With them were friends from Xenia and Salem: The Cliff Benefield family, Gene Wathan family, the "Squeek" Pickel family and the "Buck" Oulrey family from Salem. They would fish during the week, ice down the fish, and at the end of the week all the campers pooled their fish and had a campground fish fry. The second year, they received a call from a relative that the friend "Squeek" Pickel had been shot and killed while he was planting corn on a rented farm. Many of them knew who probably shot him, but there was never an arrest or trial.

They also spent 2 weeks at Big Lake, MN at a lake resort owned by George's uncle's brother-in-law, Mr. And Mrs. Brown. While there, they took a drive along the North Shore of Minnesota. His cousin Patricia's cousin by marriage, Susan, accompanied them.

Dale had a paper route before he got his drivers license. George or Kathryn would drive him around to deliver the papers, and collect each week. After he got his driver license in 1971, he got a job at A-1 Rental in Collinsville, setting up, repairing and delivering lawn equipment. He was an expert driver, since he had been operating farm tractors with George and for George's brother, Bill. Kathryn was hired for a clerical job at the First National Bank in Collinsville, which she enjoyed greatly.

Gale participated in wrestling at High School, and in one match got a knee hurt. He came home could hardly walk, and was in much pain. He went to bed and the pain would not ease. Finally in the evening the pain was too much, and George called an ambulance because he could not get to the car, much less stand to ride in the car. George went with him in the ambulance, and Kathryn followed in the car, to the hospital in Belleville, IL. He had to have immediate surgery to repair a torn ligament. He came home and had to use crutches for a couple of weeks, and then had to be very careful for several weeks.

Dale had been dating during High School, and had settled on one that he had met at a celebration at Maryville. He graduated from Collinsville High School in 1974. While talking to a counselor, he located a cooperative program in Mechanical Engineering with General Motors Institute. The Counselor told him that no one from Collinsville had ever gotten that. He decided to try for it anyway. He was accepted, and departed for the General Motors Institute at Flint Michigan. His work periods would be at their Central Foundry at Bedford, Indiana, in Mechanical Engineering. He took the Mercury Capri, and Kathryn was really upset to see him leave.

Gale worked one summer at A-1 Rental, where Dale had worked. He saved his money, and bought a new Harley Davidson dirt motorcycle. It was later in the year when he got his knee hurt at school.

Dale rented an apartment in Bedford, IN, and moved a couple of times during his work periods at the Central Foundry. He lived in the Phi Delta Theta house in Flint, MI during class sessions.

In January 1975, George was promoted to GS-14, at the same job as Chief of the Product Assurance and Test Division, P.M. ASE. This paid $28, 651 per year, and was considered Executive level in Federal Service. From GS-14 and up the positions were highly political, and required knowing someone or being referred by a friend. He was still enjoying what he did, as he had good, loyal employees, and highly respectable superiors. He felt that his talent and education was being used at the 90 percent level.

During this time they were testing a Countermeasure system mounted on the wing of the OV-1D. The airworthiness testing was conducted at Edwards Air Force Base in California and the Grumman Test Facility, at the East end of Long Island, NY. The week before the testing was to begin on Long Island, at a restaurant near the Grumman plant at Bethpage, NY, George had a dinner with the senior Grumman engineers, the chief test pilot from Grumman, and the two Army test pilots from Edwards AFB, CA. These were Major Fred Daniloff, and Captain Kenneth Schranz. During the course of the evening, George told the Army test Pilots to take their time and not take any chances with the OV-1D, and if they had a problem to bail out and leave it. He also reiterated that their schedule to go to Ft. Rucker, AL after they finished at Long Island was flexible and not to take any chances or hurry. The aircraft was heavily instrumented, and was to perform Single Engine Stalls, to check the effect of extra pod mounted on the wing of the OV-1D and find any changes in the flight characteristics during these stalls.

The next Monday George traveled the test site on Long Island, and they could not fly due to the weather. He met with the Army test pilots, and told them again not to worry about the test schedule, just take care of themselves. It was raining when he left to for New York, and turned into snow before he got back to Bethpage, NY. The main Highways were blocked due to accidents, and he wandered through Brooklyn back streets and finally got on the Staten Island Freeway to cross the river into New Jersey, and onto the New Jersey Turnpike to Ft. Monmouth, NJ. As he got onto the Turnpike, it was freezing rain. What was normally a 1-1/2 hour drive from Newark, took 6 hours because of the packed ice on the Turnpike. He arrived at Eatontown, NJ about 9:00 PM, at a Holiday Inn where he had stayed before. He asked the desk clerk if they were closed or if he could get a room for the night. The clerk told George that he could have the run of the hotel, but the bar and restaurant was closed. He told George that the cook was there because he could not get home because of the ice storm. The cook prepared them dinner, and ate with him at the same table.

George found out later that the meal was free, because there were only three people staying for the night. He met with the Laboratory personnel about 10:00 AM the next day. Normally, he would have had the meeting at 8:00 AM, but the ice storm had resulted in a power outage. The power was still off, but he met with key personnel when they arrived for about one hour. George then went to the airport at Newark, NJ, turned his rental car in, and then flew back to St. Louis.

The OV-1D Mohawk was flown from Long Island to Fort Rucker, Alabama the end of the week for the next phase of testing. George had many friends at Fort Rucker from the past as a Test Manager. He tracked the progress, and verified the progress. On Tuesday of the following week he got a call from Frank Brand at Fort Rucker, about 3:00 PM that they had an OV-1D aircraft missing. George asked for him to call when he had additional information. When Mr. Brand called back, he told George the OV-1D had crashed near Fort Rucker, with two fatalities. George asked him more questions, but he would not answer because the next of kin had not been located. George asked him if the Tail Number was 17000. He replied, "Yes" and George told him that he knew who the fatalities were.

George immediately briefed the Project Manager, and he said, "Come on, we have to advise the Commanding General." They went to the General's office, and told him what George had just heard, and that he knew the pilots. Since this was a sensitive subject, the General told the Project Manager to get George airline tickets and an advance immediately, and that he wanted him there the next morning to investigate the crash for him. George called his secretary, and told her to get airline tickets and advance. He then called Mr. Brand and told him he would be there the next morning.

He went home and packed to leave that night for Fort Rucker. He arrived at the motel near Fort Rucker about 2:00 AM, and left a wakeup call for 6:00 AM. George met with Mr. Brand about 7:30 AM, and he had a UH-1 ready to fly them to the crash site. There were two other Officers with them. While talking to witnesses, George found that the pilots had been practicing single engine stalls, that they had finished their profiles for the day and sent the Chase Plane back to base. It then appeared that they had attempted another stall at about 3000 ft altitude, and they had gone into a flat spin, which is very probable in a single engine stall. The aircraft had "Pancaked" in. In other words it landed flat with a spinning motion. It appeared that the ejection seats had been deployed, either too late or as a result of the impact. It was standard practice, not to attempt this maneuver unless their altitude was at least 5000 ft. when they retrieved the aircraft for normal flight, and certainly without a chase plane. It will never be known what the Pilot's intention was, and why he attempted that maneuver in those conditions.

When they returned to Cairns Army Airfield, George had a call from the Base Safety Officer that he wanted to talk to him. When George walked into his office, he immediately accused him of pressuring the pilots to finish the test. George replied to him that the pilots were personal friends, and to the contrary, he had told them to be careful, not to hurry, and to pay particular attention to safety. The Safety officer continued to rant, and George finally told him that if he wanted to take that approach, he would call his Commanding General, and file charges on him that would end his career abruptly. He then settled down and George asked what experience he had in testing, and if he was a qualified OV-1 Pilot. He replied negative to both questions, and George requested that if the Investigation Board had any questions, to advise him. Also, that the Project Manager desired to receive a copy of the Accident Report as soon as it was complete. George returned to Cairns field and called his Project Manager about the meeting.

He told George that he did the right thing, and if the Safety Officer gave him any trouble, he would take appropriate action against him.

George had a Mercury Marquis for a couple of years that he traded for a new Chevrolet Caprice. The Supervisor at the Central Foundry told Dale that they didn't want to see that "Foreign son-of a-bitch on their lot," meaning the Mercury Capri he was driving. He called George, and George bought a Chevrolet Malibu, and had it completely overhauled and painted, as well as new tires. Dale came home to change cars, and was elated about the Malibu. He drove it until his graduation from GMI.

Because of the OV-1D crash, a replacement had to be located, and instrumented to finish the test. Everything kept progressing, and on one trip to Fort Rucker, George learned that a new Operational Test Board was going to be established at Fort Rucker, and if he was interested in being the Technical Advisor in it. George replied that he was interested, since he knew the Development Test Board Technical Director, Dr. James Kishi and had been instrumental in implementing the Operational Test concept. Dr Kishi had a PHD in Aerospace Engineering, had retired as a high-ranking Air Force Officer, and was qualified to fly all airplanes, both fixed wing and Helicopters. He loved flying and was very safety concerned.

1976 was a very eventful year. Besides the busy job schedule and traveling for meetings and schools, George and Kathryn took Gale with them on a vacation to California. They visited Kathryn's uncle and aunt in Campbell, CA near San Francisco, including Fisherman's Wharf and several other landmarks. To get there they went near China Lake and Edwards Air Force Base where George had made several trips to for meetings. From Campbell, CA They drove down the Coast past the Hearst Castle and very beautiful scenery, past Los Angeles and on to Cardiff by the Sea, where they visited Bob and Wilma Rohde, who they had met in Elizabeth City, NC when he was in the Navy there. They also visited George's Aunts Eva and Anne in San Bernardino, CA. His aunt Eva had some memory loss, and she was found in the desert with her auto stuck in the sand. She had been a real estate broker in San Bernardino, CA for several years On their way back, they visited Thermal and Palm Springs, CA; Ft. Bliss [El Paso] Texas, and White Sands, New Mexico. They then spent the night at Carlsbad, New Mexico and the next day they drove 14 hours across Texas to Texarkana. Gale drove part of the time, including through Dallas-Ft Worth, TX.

In 1976, George applied for certification as a Quality Engineer during open season by the California Department of Consumer Affairs, and his Project Manager fully supported him. He received his Certification as a Quality Engineer in 1977 after he transferred to the Aviation Board at Ft. Rucker, AL.

In June 1976 George received his MBA from Webster University in St Louis. For the Thesis, their group selected a housing development that they called "Websteer Homes". He had two Majors, one in Business Management and the other in Foreign Relations. Websteer Homes was a complete program from starting to the forecast growth of a home construction project. George's schedule did not allow him to attend the Graduation and the Diploma was delivered to him. George kept tracking the possibility of moving to Alabama. Whenever he had the occasion to visit Ft. Rucker, he would visit Col. Bob, the Commander/President who was organizing the Operational Test Board. While in St. Louis, he had worked on a panel to develop the Operational Test Concept. In the latter part of October the COL called George for a final interview, and that he had the referral list and George was one of the highest qualified. He had a trip planned to Ft. Rucker the first of November to review the test schedule and progress. He gathered all of his background information in preparation for the interview. When he arrived at Ft. Rucker, he reviewed the testing with the Development Test Board. When they were finished, George called COL Bob and told him he was ready for the interview. They spent about two hours together with coffee, and discussed ideas, and why George thought that he could do the best job for him. They toured the offices, including George's future office in the Headquarters area if he was selected. Of course, he could not tell George the job was his, because he had to interview the other candidates. George knew the procedure from his past experience in hiring subordinates. After he returned to St. Louis, in about one week, his Project Manager got a call from the Ft. Rucker Personnel office for a release date for George. About an hour later Col Bob called George and told him that he was the best qualified, and the job was his if he would accept it. The Project Manager went to George and discussed his release date. George told him that one of his assistants, Jerry Dettmer, was well qualified to take his place, and they agreed on the first week in December.

The Aviation Systems Command in St Louis was very good for George. In the 15 years there he advanced from a GS-7 Equipment Specialist to GS-14 Supervisory General Engineer, had received a BS degree in Aircraft Maintenance Engineering and MBA, with the help of the Veterans Administration. He had several opportunities for a GS-15 in the Headquarters at Washington, DC, but declined because of the high cost of living, and the cost to move.

The personnel officer at Ft Rucker was Frances Hyde, who did an outstanding job of assisting George on auto insurance, temporary lodging, etc. Dr Kishi's wife, Louise, owned a Real Estate business in Enterprise, AL, and George contacted her about the kind and price range of the house he would be looking for. He also contacted the Daleville Inn about renting one of their apartments. He had stayed there many times on his trips to Ft. Rucker. He also talked with Kathryn and Gale on their plans, and left it up to Gale if he wanted to transfer schools, or stay at Collinsville to graduate. He contacted a local broker to list their house in Collinsville.

On Monday, the second week in December, George reported to Ft Rucker with his Chevrolet Station Wagon. He rented the apartment at Daleville Inn, and spent three days on orientation and check in. He had a reserved parking space in front or the Headquarters Building of the Aviation Board. His office was in the Command section, with the Secretary and Executive Officer office between him and the Commander's office.

George had been a member of the Army Aviation Association, and the American Helicopter Society for several years, and continued active membership. He also joined the Fort Rucker Officer's Club. He transferred his Credit Union accounts to the Army Aviation Center Federal Credit Union, which was in a trailer on Fort Rucker and checking account to the Ft. Rucker National Bank. That was the only office the Credit Union had at that time. He also had the same high-level Security clearance, and continued to review Intelligence Reports weekly.

George's contacts were about the same as before on Development and Operational testing, which helped tremendously. Also as the senior Civilian there, he also developed training programs for all civilians, and advised Military on training courses available for them.

He spent weekends looking at houses in Enterprise, Dothan, Ozark and Daleville, and one weekend at a cookout hosted by Maj. Landon, Maj. May, and Capt Tony Jones.

Just before Christmas George had a meeting at Fort Monmouth, New Jersey, and arranged to take some annual leave at his home in Collinsville. He flew from Newark, NJ through O'Hare in Chicago, to St Louis. When he arrived in St. Louis, he rented a car to drive to Collinsville. When he arrived in Collinsville, the snow was so deep that he could not get on his driveway. Soon after he arrived, Gale asked him if he had his ticket; that he was going to Ft. Rucker with him. George replied no, but he would call

TWA and get him one if this what he wanted to do. George called the airline and obtained a ticket for Gale to return to Ft. Rucker with him.

Gale went back to Daleville, AL with him and they shared the apartment he had rented. He met several friends of George's, some having children in Gale's same age group. Gale immediately decided he liked it there and would finish his Senior Year of High School in Enterprise. He went back to Collinsville, and returned with the 69 Ford. He had a friend, Shelly Drummond who he took to Huntsville on his way back to Daleville.

Gale started the last half of his Senior year at Enterprise, AL George asked a friend at the Aviation Board, Mary Anne who had a son the same age, to ask her son to show Gale around, and introduce him at the first day of school. Afterward George asked her how it went, and she told him that he left Gale in the hallway while he went into the school office. He said when he returned, boys and girls surrounded Gale and he fit in well and didn't need any introduction.

George updated Kathryn several times each week. He found the perfect house at 304 Oakwood Drive in Enterprise, but had to wait until the house in Collinsville was sold. When riding with Louise Kishi, he happened to ask what the taxes on the house were. She replied, $200.00 and he remarked that that wasn't bad, only $2400.00 per year. She said no, that was the taxes for each year. George knew the living expenses in Enterprise were much lower than Illinois, but this was tie "Icing on the Cake". Finally, in February, Kathryn called him and told him the Broker in Collinsville had a contract on their house, and she said that it seemed the perfect house for them. He had sent Kathryn pictures of the house in Enterprise, and she agreed on it. He signed a purchase contract with the provision that he had to close the house in Collinsville. The Collinsville family received their loan approved, and they wanted to move on or before March 15, 1977.

George made a deposit on the house in Enterprise, the owners moved, and he obtained possession, and bought some furniture to live until they could move entirely They arranged for the movers to move them on March 13, 1977.

He rented a U-Haul trailer in Daleville, connected it to his Chevrolet Station Wagon and headed for Collinsville, 14 hours non-stop except for gas, meals, and pit stops. He left Gale under the care of Mary Anne and with the 69 Ford. When George arrived in Collinsville, he spent three days in the house preparing for the packers and movers. They discarded a truckload of belongings, and gave away about a half-truckload. Gale called the second day, and said the Ford quit running, and he had taken it to a local repair shop. George called the repair shop, and arranged for them to repair it, and used his credit card to pay for the repairs. The last day George thought to check the freezer in the garage, and it was full. He called some neighbors, and the food was soon gone. He defrosted the freezer just in time for the packers. They started loading the station wagon, trailer and their 75 Chevrolet Caprice. By the time the packers were finished, they had everything ready except the bed they were to sleep in that night. Early the next morning, they packed the bed sheets and disassembled the bed for the movers, and were ready to leave shortly after the movers left. While the movers were loading, they did the final cleaning as they moved the furniture out, and accomplished the final task of giving the keys to the Broker and headed to Alabama. They drove to Cullman, Alabama, where they were almost exhausted, and spent the night. Early the next morning they left the motel, and arrived in Enterprise, Alabama before noon. George had purchased a dinette set, sleeper sofa and two chairs. They bought groceries, and incidentals they needed for living until their furniture arrived. They moved their belongings from the apartment at the Daleville Inn, and turned the keys in. The next day the furniture arrived in the morning, and by the end of the day, they were ready to take up residence, and unpack the moving boxes. Being the senior civilian at the Aviation Board and the most experienced, George had the responsibility to review and provide advise on all personnel actions, set up a training program for all civilians, provide training courses for Military personnel to enhance their knowledge and career enhancement, besides reviewing all technical documents, test plans, test reports, and advising on methodology, resources and equipment for testing and instrumentation. Of course, because of the Military dominance, if Military personnel didn't like what he recommended, they would ignore it. He attended several Executive management courses at Atlanta, GA and Rock Island, IL. His primary job was to protect the Commander and staff from making serious mistakes but many did not think this was important. The Methodologists were PHD level Psychologists, which were classified as Engineering Psychologists, who had no education or experience in Engineering. They had no experience aviation or equipment testing and very little in aviation. They had been Research Psychologists, and all the training in testing was two weeks at the Test School. It would have been better if they had been classified as Research Psychologists. They had been hired before George, so he had no control over their selection. All of the division chiefs were military, except the Resources Management Division. The thing that made the job difficult was that the Military were there for a short time, two to three years. They thought they were experts when they arrived, and some of them had a negative opinion of civilians.

George participated in many social functions at the Officer's Club, NCO Club, and neighbor's home. Their neighbors, Clark and Erika were sponsors or the German Students, and since Erika was of German, descent they hosted many parties. They had the pleasure to meet Erika's brother from Germany during his visits. George was a member of the Officer and

NCO Clubs, as well as Army Aviation Association, American Helicopter Society and Association of United States Army.

On July 4, 1977 Gale took some friends to Dothan. One friend wanted to show him where he had previously lived. Going down a hill on one street, they noticed a washout where a bridge had been. The road was slick, and Gale could not stop in time, and crashed into the washout. George and Kathryn had gone to Dothan for the fireworks display, and did not know about it until they got home. Gale had the car towed to the Chevrolet dealer in Dothan, and all the passengers had to go to the hospital for treatment of minor injuries. One of the girls called her parents, and her family returned all of them to Enterprise.

He traded the Chevrolet Station Wagon for a used Cadillac Sedan Deville. In late 1977 he traded the Ford LTD for a new Toyota Corolla. In 1978 he traded the Chevrolet Caprice for a new Chevrolet Malibu after it had been wrecked in the mishap by Gale.

George's brother, Bill had been diagnosed with Colon Cancer, which was inoperable at the time the Doctors detected it. He continued to go downhill for about a year, and he made several trips to visit and try to comfort him. George had consulted the best Doctors in the USA, but they all told him it was too late and the cancer was in an inoperable location, and that they could do him no good. George was with him in the Flora Hospital on March 13, 1976 when he passed away.

In August 1978 George joined the Alabama Society of Professional Engineers, and the local Chapter in Dothan. He had previously been a member of the National Society of Logistics Engineers. The Chapter had a good active membership, and he was nominated for the Chapter President. This got him active in the State Society where he became State President in 1987. He had been attending National meetings at several locations. In the winter 1987, they hosted the National Winter Convention at Mobile, Alabama. This was the height of his enjoyment and fulfillment, as the opening Speaker. He held several other positions, including State Professional Engineers in Government Chairman, National Legislative Committee and participated in many National meetings and forums.

In 1977, Gale entered Auburn University in pre-architecture, and struggled the first couple of quarters. He had an Art class, which he really enjoyed. He then decided to go into Industrial Design, one reason being the lights never went off in the Architecture building, and the Architecture program did not fit his talent. He had also received second place in construction of a mall model competition by the St. Clair County Builders Association. In 1978, Dale needed a trailer to haul his motorcycle. George bought a trailer, and had new tires put on it, and arranged for him to have a hitch put on his car. Dale went to Enterprise, had a good visit, and went back to Bloomington, Indiana, where he had arranged with some fellow students to share an apartment during their work periods at the Central Foundry at Bedford, IN.

Back on his job, George had to travel extensively to Laboratories, Test sites, other Test Boards, and other miscellaneous activities for meetings, provide guidance on tests, and assist when possible. He would travel sometimes on Military airplanes and helicopters, both for meetings and during tests. Some times he would stay in the local Bachelors Officer Quarters when available or in Motels. He was the only one having knowledge and experience in testing advanced aircraft, subsystems, electronics, and missile countermeasures, especially on the Development side, and knew hundreds of professionals throughout the USA.

One Army Major was known for drinking a little too much was at the Officer's Club one night after work, and headed home. He got just outside of the gate, when he became sick. He pulled to the side of the road, and was leaning forward on the trunk of his car heaving, when an Enterprise

Policeman stopped and asked what was wrong. The Major replied, "I am drunk, and if I get into my car, you are going to give me a ticket." The Policeman replied, "What are you going to do?" The Major replied, "I'm going to push this son-of –a-bitch home." The Policeman said, "Lock it up and get in with me. I will take you home."

In 1978/79, George bought two apartment buildings, named "Pecan Grove Apartments" on Cottonwood road in Dothan for a tax shelter. They did most of the service, including mowing, cleaning and preparing the vacated units for renting. There were 8 apartments, and he could walk in a two-bedroom apartment to paint the interior at 8:00 AM and have it finished at 4:00 PM to clean up. They also did the raking of leaves, and gathered pecans that were left, since there were several large Pecan trees on the property.

In 1979, they went to Flint, Michigan to attend Dale's graduation from General Motors Institute. They really enjoyed it. For his Thesis Project, Dale designed, developed and installed a robot system for die-casting at the Bedford plant. He bought a new Chevrolet Camero Z-28 at factory cost and sold the Chevrolet Malibu. He took a job at Union Electric in St Louis, Missouri as a field service Engineer and rented an apartment in South St, Louis. Missouri. He married Nancy on May 10, 1980 who he had been dating since High School and who had graduated from Miami University, majoring in Microbiology. George sponsored the Rehearsal Party at Char's Restaurant in Collinsville. He showed slides of the early years of Dale, and then gave the projector and screen, along with a 35mm camera to Dale and Nancy. They attended the wedding in Caseyville, just south of Collinsville. Later, George received a call from Dale. He said, "Guess what?" Knowing Dale, it was something important. He said, "some SOB stole my Z-28 last night." He obtained a rental car from the insurance company for about a month. He then called and said he had bought a new Toyota Corolla to replace the Z-28. What a change! Later Dale and Nancy bought a house in Collinsville, where they lived several years. He had worked for Union Electric for about three years, when he called and told George there was a good promotion available, but he didn't think he had much of a chance. George told him to go for it anyway, that he wouldn't get if he didn't try. He called a couple of weeks later, and told them he got it. He said he went to school for five years to be an Engineer and worked as an engineer less than four years, and after this promotion he would never work as an Engineer again. He was then an Industrial Relations Manager. He later built a new house North of Edwardsville, IL.

George and Kathryn were making many trips to Dothan to care for the apartments, and decided to move to Dothan. One tenant in the apartments operated a nightclub in Dothan, and another tenant related that she got some mail for them, and when she went to the door, a young girl greeted her nude, and appeared to be high on something. They were always late on rent, had piled used mattresses outside the side door and One night one of the brothers lost his key, and borrowed a hammer from another tenant to break a window. This went along for a month, and couples were observed coming to the apartment at night, staying about 30 minutes each, for about 31/2 hours. George decided to cancel their lease, and sent them a registered letter. They refused the letter, so he left Kathryn at the apartments, and went to the record shop one of the brothers owned. He approached him, and told him that he had refused the letter, so he was delivering it in person. He replied that his brother did not break the window, and he would remove the old mattresses when he got good and ready. He said they intended to renew their lease and stay there. George told him no, that their lease was cancelled. After he got home that night, the other tenant called and asked what he had done. He asked "Why?" and she said, "

They had two trucks, and were moving out." He told her "Good" and what he had done that day.

Two days later, he went to inspect the apartment, and found it filthy. The refrigerator had been turned off, the power had been disconnected, and there was spoiled liver and fish in the freezing unit. He had to get the power turned on, clean and deodorize the carpet, repaint the apartment, and clean and deodorize the refrigerator. He spent about $300.00 to get the apartment ready to re-lease, and the former tenant had the nerve to ask for his deposit back. George refused, and he said he would meet him in Court. George told him that he would look forward to that.

In November 1979, they purchased a four-bedroom house in Dothan, at 2903 Tarboro St. It had a wet bar, and they used one of the bedrooms for an office, which opened out to a patio on the rear.

Shortly later, George's parents in Illinois made several trips to Dothan, and liked the area very much. . They stayed for six weeks with George, and really enjoyed their visit. After that, his father's health had deteriorated with an enlarged heart, and congestive heart failure. George's brother, Bob took him to Carle Clinic in Champaign, Illinois, where they inserted a catheter to relieve the fluid buildup. George went to Illinois when he returned from Carle Clinic, and he seemed better. The only problem was that he hated hospitals and Doctors, and would not follow their directions. If a Doctor asked him if he was allergic to and medications, he would reply, "All of them."

George's father had sold his farm in Clay County, IL, but he still yearned to go back there when the weather improved in the springtime.

On one trip to Dothan, with Bob driving, George was not at home and they stopped at a nearby motel They left a message on George's phone to come down there as soon as he returned. Bob had obtained his Dad some Oxygen, and he was having breathing problems. He wanted to go to

George's house and sit on the patio. After about 15 minutes he wasn't doing better, so George told him he had to go to the hospital. He didn't resist, and George took him to the emergency room. He was really impressed with the efficiency, and afterward when he felt bad in Illinois, he would call Bob and tell him to take him to Dothan.

The latter part of March George's Mother wrote him a letter, and told him to find them a house in Dothan, that they wanted to move to Dothan near a good hospital. Also they loved the warm climate. George and Bob located the perfect house for them on Denton Road, a block from North Oates [the main thoroughfare, old US 231 North] in Dothan.

Bob went to Illinois in early April, and returned with a truck loaded with their parents' belongings. They had bought some furniture for the house, and had it ready to move into when they returned. They closed the house transaction, and their parents loved the house, location and everything about it. Just before the closing, George and Bob told them that they would buy the house for an investment, and rent it to them for just enough to pay the payments, taxes, and insurance and any upkeep. His father said, "No way. This is my house, and I am going to own it myself." They planned to assume the loans on the house for from 4.4 % to 6.00%, and their Father said " I have never paid payments on a house in my lifetime, and I am going to pay off the loans". As he had sold most of his farmland earlier, and had CD's yielding 17 to 22 percent, so they told him it was like business, that he was selling his money for 17 percent, and buying it for 4.5 to 6.00 percent, so his minimum profit was a minimum of 11 percent. He understood that, and changed his mind, but he insisted on the house being owned by him.

While in Dothan, their Father loved to watch the squirrels, and remarked that he had hunted them all his life, and learned more about them there than ever before. Their parents really enjoyed their home, and the social activities and friendliness of neighbors and friends.

In August, Gale married Phyllis of Geneva. She was a lovely lady who had graduated from Auburn University in Elementary Education. Dale was there for the wedding. They purchased a Mobile Home, and had it delivered to Auburn. Gale was driving the Toyota Corolla, and Phyllis drove a Chevrolet and did her practice teaching near Lanett, Alabama. She later got a position at Smith's Station, Alabama, in an Elementary School.

Dale married his high school sweetheart, Nancy in Collinsville on May 10, 1980. They lived in an apartment in south St. Louis, MO. Gale and Phyllis, Kathryn and George all attended the wedding.

George's father continued in Doctor's care. On October 2, 1981 his mother called to tell him that his father could not get up out of his chair, and she needed some help. George went to their house, and found his father very weak, and called an ambulance to take him to the hospital. George arrived the same time as the ambulance, and checked him in. They took him to CCU, where he seemed to be resting comfortably. George went home that night, and about 4:00AM the nurse called him and told him that his Dad was asking for him and he should come to the CCU. He was dressing, when the nurse called again and told him his Dad was still asking for him and he should come right away. He hurried to get dressed and arrived at the CCU to find his Dad seemingly resting comfortably. After he was there with him about 5 minutes, he wanted help with the bedpan that he needed to urinate. When they got the bedpan adjusted, he went limp, and blood pressure went flat. The nurse was in there immediately, and George left the CCU and waited in the waiting room. He called Kathryn, and told her to go to his Mom's house to be with her. In about 20 minutes the nurse, came to the waiting room ant told him she was sorry, that Dad had passed away, and gave him a hug. He waited about

30 minutes, and decided that Kathryn should be at his mother and he had to let them know. He called his mother, and Kathryn had not arrived, but he felt he had to tell his mother. He told his mother he would be there after he had talked to the Doctor and Undertaker. The Doctor asked George if his father had any Cancer insurance, and he replied, "No, why do you ask?" He said that he knew he had Cancer, because he had seen it, but his heart was so bad that it was useless to operate. Shortly after he arrived at his Mom's house, his Aunt Oneida and family from Centralia, IL arrived, and he had to tell them it was too late. They took his Dad to Illinois, where they had a visitation at Frank-Bright Chapel in Flora, with burial in Odd Fellows Cemetery in Xenia, Illinois. George, and Bob were named Executors of their father's Estate. They talked to their mother about the distribution of assets, and divided it as they all agreed to. George invested his part in Tax Exempt Bonds, returning a good interest rate. Most had coupons for the interest to clip and deposit in the bank. They were eventually redeemed because the interest rate was dropping. George purchased his father's car, because he needed anther vehicle.

Back at the job, George had a very busy schedule, keeping abreast the test projects, traveling to test sites to assist, and flying in Army airplanes and helicopters on test projects. He had three occasions to fly with Army Aviators in the flight simulators at Ft Rucker. One asked him, after he had taken the controls, where he learned to fly helicopters, and George told him about his Navy experience. He was elated, and told George that he should have pursued a flying career.

George was selected for a special Tri-Service Working Group by an Army Colonel from Huntsville to assist in development, acquiring, and testing foreign threat systems. This was a cloak and dagger operation, working with the CIA, FBI, as well as other top-level intelligence experts. This required various meetings, and visiting Test Sites/conducting tests at various locations. The most interesting, was at the Nevada Test Site, where everything was highly classified and very sensitive. When they left the Metropolitan Airport for the Test Site, the side curtains were pulled down in the airplane, so only the Pilot/Co-Pilot could see outside and no one could see who was in the airplane. Most were workers at the test site, because there were no living accommodations nearby. When they landed at the Test Site, the visitors were escorted to a van with black curtains over the windows and transported to the Headquarters Building. Every one was called and introduced by first name only. These included Military Generals, Colonels, and other officers, as well as high-ranking civilians and lower grades. George had the occasion to visit the Threat Museum, where they had many missile launchers, and foreign military equipment. Also there was a Russian MIG-25, which they could inspect. It was surprising, that the MIG was reasonably crude as compared to the US Jet Fighters. It had a NATO Standard fuel fill, which they were told was standard on all Russian Aircraft. There are very few persons that have or will ever visit this Museum. Later, they flew a CH-47 with George acting as Crew Chief, from Indian Springs Air Force Base to the test site for testing countermeasures against actual threat systems. Here during a waiting period, the Air Force Thunderbirds were practicing maneuvers. At the test site, they saw Air Force fighters practicing maneuvers against foreign fighters. If the foreign fighters had a problem, the all non-essential personnel were herded into a brick building with no windows, until the problem was over. During these visits, there were other duties that can never be related. One thing can be related, was a MIG-25 flying for something like "Top Gun" training. These included counter-espionage, and undercover activities, which he was not particularly proud of, but were necessary in that area, by selected personnel including him. He had previously participated in some undercover operations, which he can never discuss locations or dates with anyone.

The high point in this assignment was getting exposed to the cutting edge of technology. The Colonel that requested George was so busy traveling, that he would go to an airport and ask them when the next plane left. The desk clerk asked where he desired to go, and he would reply, "That doesn't matter. I just want the next flight." Due to security, he wouldn't let anyone know when or where he was going. He kept his own schedule and traveled most of the time, due to the high security classification of projects. He sensed that sometimes he was being followed, and he tried to evade them in any way possible. Participants in the group were changed about every year, probably so they wouldn't be recognized for their participation.

Anne, the Command Secretary, was surprised when a Memory Typewriter was delivered to her. After it was set up and she tried it, she told Col Bob that "He could shove it where the sun didn't shine," and she would quit over that. After she became more acquainted with it, she settled down, and after a few weeks passed, she loved it. While on the subject of Anne, she was in tears many times when the Col. almost demanded that she go home with him when his wife was out of town.

George had flight gear stored in his file cabinet, because at any time he would need it to fly in Military aircraft. This consisted of fire retarding flight suit, gloves, helmet and combat boots. One day he needed the gear for a flight, and the combat boots were missing. He called Security, and reported it. The Military investigator accused him of taking them for his personal use. He told him that he had no personal use for them, and that some Military person had taken them. He wrote a report, but never questioned any Military person about them.

While George was at the Aviation Board, he heard the term "God Damn Civilian" more times than he could keep track of. Looking back, He says that if the TRADOC system and the Army was interested in keeping highly educated and experienced talent, instead of backstabbing senior civilians and attacking them, the entire system would be better managed. Some way could have found to promote and recognize him and could have been done if the respect for professionalism was better. The development community, which was dominated by civilians, treated advancing and senior civilians with respect and dignity and supported them fully. George said he realized after 3 or 4 years at the Aviation Board, that his career was at a dead end. However, the priority of family and the lower living costs in Alabama were the bonuses and these considerations probably overrode the possibilities of moving again and accepting higher-level positions. George found that the only information to the Military news media was good news. There were a lot of underlying factors that the public will never know, and in some cases, should not know.

George attended several Executive Seminars and courses at Rock Island Arsenal, Illinois and Atlanta, Georgia. He was told before he left, to learn all he could, but "Don't dare come back here and try to implement any of that Bull Shit." George realized that use of his education and training was deteriorating, to about 60 percent and to about 10 percent when his health failed and he took his disability retirement.

George received four offers to for a promotion in Washington, DC, but turned them down, because of the cost of living in the DC area and family concerns about moving to DC. While at Ft Lee, VA, he went for an interview at a senior civilian's home in Washington DC.

The Colonel was observed cashing in Iranian vouchers at the Dothan airport for commercial flights. He had spent a tour of duty in Iran, and was close friends to the Shah. They had several gifts from the Shah in their home.

On one occasion George had a trip planned to the Air Defense Board at Ft. Bliss, Texas. Charley French was his counterpart there, and Colonel Crosby was the Commander. On Monday morning, about 3 hours before departing from the Dothan airport, he got a call from Colonel Crosby. He told George that he had an appointment with the Commanding General of Ft Bliss to explain a message he had seen from the Aviation Board. George's orders were on Colonel Bob's desk. When he told him about the conversation with Colonel Crosby, he went in orbit. He said, "Godammit, George, you will never talk to a General Officer under any circumstances. They are all liars and crooks." George told him that he should call the Colonel at Ft. Bliss and tell him that. He said no for George to call and cancel the meeting, and he would tear up the orders. George told him to go ahead that he needed to make a phone call. He asked George who to, and he told him never mind, that he knew people higher than him or any General, and he should prepare to vacate the Post, because after he made the call, his career was over, and he would be told to vacate in 24 hours. After arguing for about 30 minutes, he decided for George to go ahead. George was late and had to stop at his home to get his luggage on the way to the airport. Kathryn could tell he was upset when she took him to the airport. He went to Ft. Bliss, and the next morning, Colonel Crosby escorted him to the General's office. Several of the General's Directors were present, and he had a good discussion with the General, and answered all his questions. The General asked about the Ft. Rucker Flight Simulators, and after George explained how the aviation simulators operated, the General then told his Director of Training to make sure George was briefed on their Air Defense Simulators before he left. George was briefed on the simulators, and then given a demonstration. It was a terrific experience. As soon as he could, he called Colonel Bob and reported on the meeting. The Colonel said, "Thanks, George. I knew you would do well." George thought, "You crazy SOB. After the harassment you put me through and then make such a statement." On March 1982 Brandon Blake was born to Gale and Phyllis, in Auburn, AL. Kathryn and George were there, but Kathryn had to take George to the airport in Montgomery, Alabama, to leave for a business trip. Kathryn went back to the hospital in time for Brandon to be born.

In 1982, George traded the Cadillac for a new Oldsmobile Delta 88 Diesel. In 1980, Bob had introduced him to the Elks Lodge in Dothan. He joined and was very active because of the outstanding members of the Lodge.

In June of 1982 Gale graduated from Auburn University, with a B.S degree in Industrial Design. Phyllis graduated a year earlier, and taught on year at an Elementary School at Smith Station, Alabama. When they were married, they had bought a new Mobile Home. After Graduation they sold the Mobile Home, Gale accepted a job at Reliable Metals in Geneva, Alabama and they rented a house in Geneva, Alabama. Phyllis obtained a teaching position in Geneva, and they were on their way. After a while, An independent sales agent in Louisville, KY, who met Gale at Reliable Metals Co, called asked him to start a company, which they named American Leisure Designs. He resided with Tom Kneipshield in Louisville, KY for a while as they were organizing. They rented industrial space at Georgetown, Kentucky, and Gale rented an apartment in Lexington, Kentucky. Gale developed the company from the ground up, buying a desk, chair and computer. At one time, he installed the bleachers in the U.S Navy Memorial in Washington, DC. Also, at that time he purchased George a "plank" in the Navy Memorial.

In the summer of 1982, Kathryn, George and Gale, Phyllis and baby Brandon attended the Worlds Fair in Knoxville, TN, and dined on top of the Space Needle. This was an experience none of them will ever forget

On March 26, 1983 Michael Patrick was born to Dale and Nancy. In June 1983, George was initiated into The Order Of The Engineer, an elite society, pledging honesty and recognizing the importance of the Engineering profession from the beginning of time. Anyone could recognize the

Order member, by a ring on the little finger of the working hand [left or right]. Back with the Elks, George had a very busy time. He served as Inner Guard, Treasurer, on the Board of Directors, Loyal Knight, and substituted in Chairs when an officer was absent. He participated on the Committee for a State Elks Convention, and as the Chairman stated, "they didn't sleep for three days and two nights." Tickets for the Cadillac drawing to benefit the Elks Memorial Center in Montgomery totaled around $25,000 each year. The Dothan Lodge had a very active membership, and all supported the Lodge well.

During this time George noticed the Operational Test concept in Aviation going downhill. The Aviation Board aviators were so aggressive to get flight time, that instead of an Operational Unit getting most of the flight time the Aviation Board aviators were using a large part of the time flying profiles, instead of the Unit Aviators. Also the Resource Management personnel were being ordered to switch Test Funds to other projects. This was the only Division that had a Civilian Chief, who was a top notch, experienced and honest supervisor in the Aviation Board. George's travel schedule was heavy. They were running a test at Fort Ord, CA, which was progressing on schedule. George went there to finish the test, planned for three days. Due to some problems with weather and other actions, he had to call back for more expense money when he discovered that his visit would be longer. He worked with a very capable female Captain who was not an aviator, but working 10 hours a day, including one weekend. He and the Captain worked the long hours to finish the test. He recycled the clothing he had taken, washing his clothes on Sunday. After 10 days, the data and reports were to the point that he could turn it over to the Captain and the Test Officer, and he returned to Fort Rucker. On one trip he made to Edwards Air Force Base, he was returning the Los Angeles Airport on a tight schedule. As he rounded a curve on the Interstate, he saw a California

Trooper approaching from the rear, so he pulled to the shoulder because he knew he was speeding. The Trooper pulled behind George, stopped, and asked if he knew how fast he was going. George told him no. He then asked him other questions, about where he had been, where he was going, etc. He gave George a ticket, which had a court appearance date. When he returned he told the Col, as a joke, that he had go back there to appear. He said, "Hell no.!" George called the Court and asked what the fine was. The clerk told him, it was $78.00. He asked her if he could mail a check to them for that amount. She said, "Sure." All the traveling he did, this was the only ticket he ever received.

About this point George saw the fallacies in the test and Military [Army], putting personal goals ahead of the original Operational Test concept. His counterpart at the Development Test Activity was ousted from his position through false accusations and unethical treatment. Dr Kishi moved to Texas, and never returned to Ft. Rucker. At various times TRADOC would get on a roll to reduce the civilian grade levels in the organization. Guess who was always the target of cutbacks? It was George, the most senior and highest paid civilian in the organization. The job should have been upgraded to GS-15, but instead of doing something positive, everything was negative, and George was continually viscously attacked because of jealousy and no one could comprehend the wide knowledge and experience and potential he had. Incidentally he passed his fiftieth birthday, and was considered "too old for the job". About this time he was being used only about 10 percent of his ability, education and training. One person told the President of another Board, that if he wanted a job with the Contractor when he retired, he had better make the system they were testing look good. He did just that, and when he retired, he had a job the next week with the Contractor. The system was later found to have some serious shortcomings that should have been uncovered during the test.

Also new Officers were assigned to the Aviation Board, attended the two-week Operational Test orientation course, and were suddenly experts. One Captain, a West Point graduate presented a test plan for review. George found many errors in it, and called him to his office to discuss the problems. After telling him some of the errors, the Captain blew up and told George that if he didn't like it, to prepare it himself. George could understand because the Captain was assigned a task he was not prepared for, and was working 14 hours a day and weekends to respond to his supervisor, who was a LTC, and accomplish the demands. George told the Colonel the problem, and that he didn't want to make a big issue, but he should talk to the Captain's superior. The Colonel told him in no certain terms, that it was none of his business, and for him to talk to the superior. This is an example of the gross disrespect on the part of the Military for professionalism and mutual respect of civilians.

Another problem was the Officer Evaluation Reports. This was a top priority of every Officer to "Max out" the report. One that George saw read, "He managed a project of great magnitude, commanding 38 military and 26 civilians, and managing over 20 million dollars" About half of these reports were false. In the first place, A Captain or Major, or any officer never commands senior civilians. They may supervise lower grades, not command. Secondly, some of the civilians out ranked the officer and therefore should not have been supervised by Military personnel. The manager of the funds for the test was a civilian, and the Test Officer just spent or wasted the funds. Thirdly, he didn't even supervise near that many Civilians, and most of the Military were commanded by the using activity Commander, and consequently could not have been commanded by the Project Officer. It was noticed that the Generals, Colonels and Lt Colonels would command their troops in Military actions, but had no control in this type of environment, which was termed TDA [Table of Distribution and Allowances]. Military personnel in an environment such as this, with Military dominance, don't want to accept the fact that most Civilians are more experienced in their fields and should be respected. George was continually bypassed on various actions, because there was continuing disrespect for education, training and experience.

Another fallacy was that because the unit used Research and Development funds for test projects that this assignment counted as Research and Development experience. This was not the case for most officers and civilians, because most were not educated as engineers, and they could not even comprehend the efforts that went on up to 10 years before the Operational Tests in the Research and Development community. Thus, the few that that had spent many years in the Research and Development community were disrespected and ignored.

George had submitted the forms for the Federal Engineer Of The Year, and in February 1984, he received a call that he had been selected as The TRADOC Federal Engineer of the Year, and all expenses would be paid for him and Kathryn to go to Washington, DC to receive the award. On February 22, they flew to Dulles Airport, and took a Limo to the hotel. There they were given time to freshen up, and proceeded to the Hotel Ballroom. Here they had a reception, then dinner at 7:00PM, with some Colonel Adams and other Colonels from Headquarters At Fort Monroe, VA, and Herb Koogle, the President of the National Society of Professional Engineers. Afterward, George was presented the Award. The hotel room cost was $128.00, which was the highest priced hotel he had ever been in. George had met Mr. Koogle before at National meetings he had attended as the Alabama representative. George was very active at the National level for several years, attending meetings in Washington, DC; San Francisco, CA, Buffalo, NY; Albuquerque, New Mexico; Denver, CO; Los Angeles, CA; Indianapolis, IN; New Orleans, Louisiana, and Dallas, TX. He also served as the Alabama State Chairman of the Professional Engineers in Government, and was a member of the National Legislative Committee. During 1984 and 1985, the Colonel, behind his back, tried to eliminate George's position. The disrespect for professionalism continued to erode and some others related that he wanted to place a retired Lt Colonel in that job. However George fought it and won, once meeting with the Commanding General. Because he objected, the Colonel and possibly others started using Management Subversion techniques. George found a paper that had been presented in a course at Ft Leavenworth, Kansas. [This is appended here as Appendix D]. He never discussed the subject with George. At this point, it appeared George was over qualified for the position he was in and was grossly underutilized. Since then, George realizes that there is widespread discrimination due to age. An article in the VFW magazine in November 2005 described the lack of opportunity for military retirees to obtain Civil Service vacancies because they were too old. Although this discrimination was outlawed many years ago, it is still practiced. George was the Alabama state chairman of Professional Engineers in Government in 1984 and 1985. He attended most State meetings for ASPE. During at least two occasions he had the pleasure of meeting and having breakfast with U.S Senator Howell Heflin.

In 1985, He sold the apartments on Cottonwood Rd. in Dothan to an investor from Abbeville, AL. The problems with the management were becoming more difficult because of the quality of tenants they were experiencing.

His mother was really enjoying the social aspects of the South. She loved her home, and was a good mixer at many social functions.

Colonel Bob finally retired, upon the insistence of the Commanding General. He moved to Atlanta, GA, because he was in so much trouble, he was not welcome at Fort Rucker. He was replaced with a top notch Commander, Colonel Grett, who was a good supervisor and Commander. The Aviation Board had gone too far downhill, for Col. Grett to recover it. In summary, the Military wanted to run the organization like an active Army Unit. This was not the case with a Civilian makeup.

When George reported to Ft. Rucker in December, 1976, there was a Major, named Anthony "Tony" Jones, who with Major Bill May hosted him for a cookout one Sunday before Kathryn joined him. They were super officers, and Tony Jones and he became good friends, and worked well together. The next time George heard of Tony was 1999 or 2000, when he returned to Ft Rucker as Post Commander. He was then a Major [two-star] General.

While George was at Ft. Rucker, he met many fine officers and Enlisted Men and women who were very professional. There were only a few that were bad, and they got or will get their reward eventually.

In the last part of 1985 and first part of 1986, the Aviation Board was going downhill, and no one seemed to care. George had many tasks piled on him, and there was a decreasing amount of coordination, and fulfilling the purpose he was there for. He was under a Doctor's care for high blood pressure. He started having blackouts while driving, and consulted his doctor. The Doctor found that he was under severe pressure, and his blood pressure was fluctuating. The Doctor called the Colonel, and told him that George would not be back, and asked George what his options were. He told him that he could retire on disability, if he would support him in the process.

The Civil Service Regulations provided that if an employee became disabled to perform their current job, at their current Grade Level, they were entitled for Disability Retirement. George went to the Civilian Personnel Office at Fort Rucker, and obtained the forms for Disability Retirement, and cleaned his office of personal items. He took the Doctor statement to his Doctor, and he completed his part. George completed the rest of the paper work, and forwarded the package to the Civil Service Commission. He had almost one year of sick leave accumulated, and had to use that up before his retirement could be effective. Also, the Aviation Board could not replace him at least until the retirement was effective. By the time he had used his sick leave, he would be only a little over one year from regular retirement.

The application for disability was rejected, wanting more information. Dr. Jones prepared more justification, and recommended he see a Psychiatrist. George made an appointment with the Psychiatrist recommended. He interviewed him for 30 minutes, and then said, "You are very intelligent, and not crazy, but I know what the Government system was like, so I will prepare a report that should get you through." George never read the report, but the second package he submitted was approved. It is a crime that the Civil Service Commission would spend thousands in resources to deny a request such as this, and demonstrating a negative approach.

Some of the best people George had the pleasure to work for/with in St Louis were Conrad Busse, William Hassell, Jack Lucky, Col Luther Jones, Col. Solar, Col Newton, Col Keaton, Col Shirey, and BG/MG Billy Bunker, the finest and most intelligent Commander of the Aviation Command he ever knew in St. Louis. The General had a memory that was unusual, and made it a practice to know everyone in his Command by first name and last name. Once after the General was reassigned to Washington, DC as a Major General, he and his wife were at the Officer's Club at Ft. Lee, VA, where George and other students went for breakfast. There were four from St Louis, and the General arose, went to the table, addressed each one from St. Louis by first name and asked how things were at St. Louis. Some of the clerical personnel George had the pleasure to work with in St. Louis were, Claudia Hassell, Joan Leopold, and Deborah Tregoning who married Mike Hoffman, an Engineer who worked in the Engineering Directorate.

At Ft Rucker, George had many friends, including Mary Anne Ellis, Ann Casky, Sue Phillips, Bobby Tindall, Dr. VanLoo, Dr James Dees, LTC Rhodes, LTC Bill May and Maj. Tony Jones [who was a Major General the next time he was heard of when he returned as Commanding General of Ft Rucker]. As a comparison, George's gross salary in 1986 would be comparable to about $110,000.00 per year in 2004, according to the Federal Employees Almanac. The retirement at the same grade and step level in 2004 would be more than $15,000.00 more than George's retirement, because the COLA [Cost of Living Allowance] has not kept up with the actual increase in cost of living.

In 1985, George traded the Oldsmobile Diesel for a new GMC Conversion Van. He was traveling to Birmingham, Alabama monthly to the ASPE Board meetings.

In 1986, George was elected President-Elect of the Alabama Society of Professional Engineers. He attended a National meeting in Indianapolis, Indiana that summer. He needed something to do without earning a salary, so he organized and incorporated Dothan Nut Company, Inc. He had custom bags, a bag sealer, and would buy raw peanuts in bulk at Dothan and sell through National publications. He wanted to offer prepared peanuts and pecans, but could not get any help for experimentation. His mother had helped his brother and him to buy eight acres south of Dothan, which had a house for Bob to reside in while he was organizing bottled water and water distiller business as the place had a block building they converted into office space.

George's retirement was effective in December 1986. At this point, he had dedicated more than 29 years to public service, and donated an average of 102 hours per month for the past 20 years, taking work home on weeknights and weekends, as well as when traveling. This resulted in many hours he never got paid for, nor did he expect to be paid for. He considered this part of the job. The donated time equaled about five years. The Ft Rucker Personnel Officer related during the application for retirement, that not to underestimate the value of it. She informed him that at his level, the retirement and benefits were valued at more than one million dollars. Thus, the dedication to duty was a waste of effort. George, as a result of his experience, has lost faith in the Army, the Civil Service System and Government in general. He learned how the different levels of Governments operate, and has said, "Government at all levels do and relate what is politically correct, and which may be or not be ethically or morally correct.

CHAPTER V

Business Venture

In December, his brother Bob and he went to Atlanta, Georgia to the Recreational Vehicle Show, because they had been considering selling Travel Trailers. They had previously remodeled the block building, erecting a wall between the office area and parts area. They also installed carpeting and new wall panels in the office area. Three desks, file cabinets and brochure racks were also installed. George bought a lighted sign with letters for the front area of the lot. They met a representative from Shasta, and decided to pursue this business if they could get floor plan financing. Mr. Boyd from the plant in Longview, Texas came to their lot and assisted in completing the necessary paperwork for dealership and financing, both floor plan and retail. A lady named Liz was the clerk for both him, and Bob. Bob was building a water and water distiller business. Christmas day, and soon after January1987 they received five new Shasta travel trailers. The reason they decided to go into this business, was there was only one Coachmen dealer in Dothan, and the nearest nearby Recreational Dealers were two in Panama City and one in Level Plains, Alabama, near Enterprise. They thought there was room for honesty and professionalism in business. Bob went to Coachmen in Indiana for service training, and he handled service and George handled all the business arrangements and sales. He changed Dothan Nut Co Inc., Inc to Quality RV Sales, Inc. He started out floor plan financing with Chrysler First in Chicago, and retail financing with John Deere Finance Co. in Iowa. The latter part of 1987 he received a call from John Deere, asking if he was interested in selling repossessed units for them. He replied yes, and the last of 1987 and 1988, and 1989 they picked up motor homes and travel trailers in Florida as far south as Key West, North Carolina, Minnesota, Georgia, Alabama, and Illinois. They sold about 40 units for them, and had as many as 23 units at one time. Quality RV would pay the expense of picking them up, cleaning them, and repairing any defects.

Bob had received an ultimatum from his wife in Illinois, and when he would not comply, she divorced him. Some childhood neighbors, Larry, Carl and Kelly began working for them in service and the business was growing. Larry became interested in a lady up the highway that had been recently divorced, and had a Beauty Shop in her home. He found another job, and eventually married the lady. Bob was busy in his water business, and he hired a housekeeper. She soon moved in with him in an extra bedroom. She started talking to truck drivers on the CB and inviting them to stop. She also told that she went to their office, and George had the door locked with Liz on the sofa in the parts room. This was a pure lie, and she started telling other lies on George and Bob. Liz became upset because of her lies. In 1988, they were looking for another line, and started selling Viking pop-ups, and Sprinter and Sport travel trailers made by Mallard. They sold several Sprinter and Sport trailers. Mallard went bankrupt and they received the last fifth wheel that was not standard. It appeared that they had gathered all left over parts and installed them on it. Even the axles were different. Also the Sport travel trailers seemed all right. However Kelly was installing a Cable TV receptacle next to the door, and called George to look at it. He asked Kelly what was wrong, and he replied that it had no insulation between the walls.

George was President of the Alabama Society of Professional Engineers in 1987 and 1988. He had attended and represented the State of Alabama and the Government well at meetings for three years including Orlando, FL, Albuquerque, New Mexico, Tucson, AZ, San Francisco, CA, Washington, DC, Buffalo, NY, Denver, CO, Seattle, WA, St Louis, MO, Ft Worth, TX and Indianapolis, IN. He had the pleasure of welcoming National delegates to the winter meeting of the National Society of Professional Engineers at Mobile, AL as the President of the Alabama Society of Professional Engineers. He also was elected as Alternate National Director and was one of the few voting on National issues at the National Conventions. George was the first and only member of the Southeast chapter of ASPE ever to be elected to President of ASPE.

Quality RV had expanded their sources for retail financing, and changed floor plan finance to a company in Atlanta, which was Chrysler First and later was purchased by Duetsch Bank and renamed Duetsch Finance. In the last part of 1988, a Suburban pulled into the Quality RV lot, pulling a travel trailer they had never seen before. The man introduced himself as David, the President of a new Manufacturing Co, and had just started building travel trailers in 1988. They looked it over, liked what they saw, and asked him what their cost would be on a 30 ft front kitchen. When he gave them the figure, they liked it even more. It was lower than any other comparable models of the same kind. It seemed superior quality, and was attractive. He was on his way to Florida to deliver that trailer, and told them he would like for them to be a dealer for his product. George told him that he had to his get floor plan increased, and he would see him at the show in Louisville, KY. George also asked him what territory they could have and he told them that there would not be any other dealer within 100 miles. He had one in Columbus. GA and planned one for Pensacola, FL and Birmingham, AL. At Louisville, George ordered five units. George hired Gene Johnson as salesman in 1988, and they both went to the RVIA show in Louisville, KY the last of November 1988. They were outgrowing their office space in the block building, so George purchased a two-room portable building and put it in front of the block building. Gale, who had moved his business to Greenville, AL designed and built two aluminum steps for the building. George hired a specialist to provide and install an air conditioner with a heating unit in the building. This provided office space for George, Kathryn as clerical in one room, and Gene in another room. A visitor who had moved from the Northeast, to Florida stopped and asked if they would consider selling his 1986 Ford F-350 diesel and Avion travel trailer. They needed a tow vehicle, and George told him to bring it to the lot and they would sell them for him. They were also still selling some repossessions and a few consignments, and the business was increasing. In about a week the man brought his F-350 and his Avion travel trailer for Quality RV to sell for him. When he arrived, George was on the phone with a dealer in Texas trying to locate a tow truck. He hung up the phone and greeted him. George started to complete the consignment agreements, and told him Quality RV needed the truck, and would like to buy the truck and sell his trailer. He agreed, and George asked him what he thought the truck was worth. He asked his opinion, and George told him he would pay $14,000 for the truck. He agreed, and George asked him to go to the bank with him. He had already discussed it with the Bank President, and called to make an appointment. The man had the title, and George arranged with the bank to give him a check, and the customer signed the title. Now they had their Tow Truck, a 1986 Ford F-350 long bed pickup with a towing package, load leveling hitch and had 56,000 miles on it.

George and Gene went to the RVIA show in Louisville, KY. They drove the Ford Dually and George purchased a travel trailer and mini-motor home to save transportation costs, and returned them to the Quality RV lot. George also purchased a sign with the new manufacturer's logo and installed it on an elevated pole about 15 feet high.

George sold his GMC van and used the truck for everything, including pick up of repossessed units, delivering sold units, and general lot use.

Business was increasing rapidly. They had all the pine trees cut on the property, to avoid the trees or limbs falling on the units. They also purchased hitch locks for the travel trailers and fifth wheels to deter thefts. They refinanced the property and remodeled the house into office space. They had a shop built on the end to provide shelter for service. They also had a chain link fence installed, with two gates for entry, and also spread rock on the drive to reduce dirt and dust. They purchased a tractor, blade and mower, and also fabricated a hitch so that they could tow trailers around the lot.

Also they needed about 100 feet on the side of the property, tapering off to about 10 feet. They leased the extra property from the lady that owned the property next to them.

Quality RV sold a fifth wheel camper to a customer in California, who had visited the lot earlier when he was on vacation. He called one Sunday afternoon, told George exactly what he wanted, and asked them to price it out and call him back. When George called him back, he told the customer that they wanted to save him enough to pay for his trip back to Alabama. He was given the price, which had a decent profit for Quality RV. He them told George to order it and he would overnight a deposit. About a month later the trailer was delivered to Quality RV. They called him and told him they were servicing it, and they needed two days before it was ready. Quality RV prepared the necessary documents for his Credit Union, and received a check for the balance owed by Federal Express. About a week later, the customer arrived at the lot, and the service department installed his hitch and electrical hookup. George was on a trip when he picked it up, but his salesman, Gene Johnson handled it well. Later he the customer was called to see if he was satisfied, and asked him if Quality RV saved him enough for the trip. He replied they saved him enough to stay in Holiday Inns and have good meals, all truck expenses, and quite a bit of money left to spare. He thanked them for the professionalism exhibited in the transaction.

Another customer from Anchorage, Alaska, who was in the Army stationed there, dealt with them by phone and Fax, and Quality RV handled the documents with the Credit Union in Anchorage. They came to the lot to pick up the trailer, and get their hitch and electrical hookup installed.

During the winter months Kelly converted the house into office and parts space. George had carpet laid on the floors and purchased three more desks and chairs. Also he purchased a copier, file cabinets and a cash register. Quality RV expanded their parts stock and hitch inventory.

Quality RV had several trespasses and thefts. When they were in the temporary building, the damage was limited to broken windows. After moving into the former house, they had a break-in where someone broke in the back door, and stole the cashbox, which had about $120 and two Bank Money Orders totaling about $20,000 from a bank in Canada for two units sold to Canadian customers. The Money Orders were replaced, but they never located the moneybox and cash. On another occasion, a new color TV for giveaway at the RVDA Open House was stolen. Someone broke in and stole the new TV, another used color TV, and a VCR. Later they had the corner of the fence cut, and there as a new a pop-up slide-in camper that someone had spent the night in, had empty and unopened beer cans, and potato chips scattered all over the interior. The intruder had also used the bath stool, which was not connected to any drain. It had rained the night before, and they thought it might have been a vagrant who got caught in the rain and sought shelter. Also, they had a generator stolen from a consigned Motor Home. This was suspected to have occurred during the influx of "Irish Travelers" commonly called Gypsies, who were living about 2 miles from Quality RV, kept Quality RV personnel all busy for a time. The worst occurrence was in 1995, which will be discussed later.

In January 1992, George's mother had open-heart surgery to replace a defective valve she had since a child. He spent two nights and two days in the waiting room, during the surgery and recovery room. She spent about a week in the hospital then went to Gran's Home, an assisted living facility for care for several months. She also had a pacemaker installed. George had to obtain a second mortgage on her house to pay the expenses. After about three months she returned to her house, and had the pacemaker checked weekly by telephone.

Dothan Camper Sales, which had been owned by "Pat" Patton, a good friend of George, was sold to a retired schoolteacher who the District Sales Manager for Coachmen persuaded to more Coachmen units to increase sales. He didn't know much about public relations so many of their customers went to Quality RV.

Their business was still increasing rapidly, so they hired a Secretary to help with the administrative workload. George located a computer system he could obtain, with 4 monitors, the software and training for personnel for $5,000.00.

The secretary hired had college training in business and computers, and was capable of using the computer and George had been trained in computer usage and programming. When George mentioned it, his partner told him that they were not getting a computer, and if he went ahead with it, she would leave him and the business. She was getting stressed because of the increase in business. In addition to bookkeeping, she had been cleaning new units and the office area. Her system of bookkeeping was using checkbook entries only. They desperately needed more depth in the bookkeeping to tell where the expenditures were going, and to find what elements of the business were profitable and which ones were unprofitable. So, they hired a bookkeeper, and bought a manual book keeping system from New England Business Supply [NEBS]. The system cost about $80.00, plus labor and overhead for the bookkeeper for eight months until she was fired for sloppy work. The cost was about $12,000.00 plus overhead, which totaled about $18,000.00. This didn't make sense, but that was necessary to keep peace in the family. George still had to keep the unit sales records and the customer database was approaching 6000 and too huge to handle manually. George was also handling advertising for the business including Television, radio, newspapers, telephone books, and had a toll free telephone number. Quality RV was severely hampered by the lack of a computer system to handle the sales and expense records, direct mail capability, and inventory records.

Carl and Kelly were trained in parts management and service to the point they were the best and the shop was fully equipped. On one occasion they both went to the Prowler plant in Longview Texas for service training. Kelly could repair, or rebuild any travel trailer or fold-down camper. George hired a service manager who had been the service and parts manager at the previous Dothan Camper Sales, which went out of business after the retired school- teacher, had sold out just before bankruptcy. Meanwhile customers were telling Quality RV that a Pensacola dealer for the same brand had set up a lot in Panama City, FL, and was stocking and selling the Quality brand. George called manufacturer, and they denied it. This went on for about a year, and he decided to see for himself. He drove to Panama City, and sure enough, Emerald Coast had a lot full of the Dutchmen units.

George called Glen at the factory and told him that he had personally seen the lot. Glen then admitted that the Pensacola dealer was selling their units at Panama City, FL, but said he couldn't do anything about it. Glen was now the President of the manufacturer, and "Cole" was the National Sales Manager.

A peanut vendor asked George if he could set up outside the front fence, and George told him ok, but if the State ran him off he couldn't do anything about it. Sure enough, the Trooper stopped and ran him off, and told him to not come back. About an hour later a State truck came and installed Right Of way signs, on the Quality RV fence line, and installed several "No Parking" signs along the Right Of Way next to the road. This had the potential to shut Quality RV down because their parking area was outside the fence, where the Right Of Way extended about 45 feet. George had past disagreements with the County Engineer, and called the District Engineer in Ozark, and told him he had it with the County State Engineer. George told him that he would give him 24 hours to remove those No Parking signs, or he was going to call the State Department of Registration and submit a complaint on the County Engineer. He didn't need him to tell George where the Right Of Way was, because George was experienced in both determining his right of way, surveying and real estate laws. The District Engineer replied that he would take care of it, because George had known him from State meetings of the Professional Engineers. The signs were removed the next morning.

Another Corp. bought the Mfg. Co. and made several changes. The manufacturer had become number one in nationwide sales. They also had been known as the best and lowest priced manufacturer of travel trailers. Some of the components were replaced, such as the electrical inverter that changed 110 volt AC to 12 volt DC and overall the units were degraded.

The Aviation Board that George had retired from was disbanded and the functions moved to Ft. Hood, Texas. Some blamed George for getting it disbanded before he retired, but he did nothing to do with getting it disbanded. In George's opinion, it was internal destruction, because of the actions previously described.

One day a potential customer drove up and stopped near the corner of the lot where the block building was that was used for the first office, and then used for parts and tool storage. George recognized the driver as a Sergeant he had known from Fort Rucker. George greeted him by name, and introduced himself as he was walking toward the block building. When George spoke to him, he was startled, rushed back to his car and sped off without saying a word. George never found out what his motive was.

Quality RV had sold a fifth wheel camper to a customer in Crestview, FL, who was a retired Air Force Warrant Officer, and knew his way around. He had problems with water leaking around the slide-out room. Quality RV did everything possible to fix it, but the hole in the side where the slide fit was not cut out square. There was no way to repair it without taking it back to the factory and rebuilding it. The customer took it to the dealer at Pensacola, FL, because that was much closer to his home. They could not fix it, as George had told the manufacturer it could not be fixed in the field. The customer forced the manufacturer to repurchase it, because of a Florida Lemon Law. It was classified as a "Lemon" according to Florida law. The manufacturer then consigned the unit to the Pensacola dealer to resell it, which should have not have been allowed. The customer that bought it from the Pensacola dealer came to Quality RV for repair for the same leaks. He was told the story about the unit, and he was sick. It was found out that the Pensacola dealer had sold it for $4000.00 more than Quality RV had sold it new to the original customer. It is not known what ever happened to it. A few months later George, and Quality RV Sales received notification that they were named to Who's Who Worldwide in 1992, life members, and to the Who's Who Worldwide Executive Club. This listed the top 30,000 individuals and Companies in the world.

Some have stated that it was nothing but a hoax, because it was "bought into." This was a lie because George never bought into anything. The only expenditures were for books and plaques. Among others it was considered an honor. The retired Air Force Warrant Officer from Florida was thought to be the one who nominated them, but no one will ever know. All they could find out was the one that nominated them was an unidentified person from Florida.

Quality RV began selling Jayco travel trailers and pop-ups for a while, as a second line. The travel trailers didn't sell well, but the pop-ups were the best available, and they sold well. After they sold out of the Jayco travel trailers, they changed to Prowler, made by Fleetwood. It sold well, and they found out from experience that the Prowlers made in Longview, Texas were much better quality than those made in Indiana.

George and his salesman, B.H. Baxley were returning from a show in Louisville, KY when they got a call from Kathryn that a used motor home they had traded for was on fire on the highway South of the lot. The other Salesman, Luke was driving it with two engine mechanics trying to see what was wrong that the engine would not run properly. They had the center console removed to adjust the timing and carburetor. About a mile south of the lot it caught fire, and Luke got it into the highway divider, got it stopped, and he and the mechanics escaped scared but uninjured. The mechanics said that they would never work on a motor home again.

In the summers of 1992 and 1993, the Pensacola dealer put on RV shows at Marianna, FL, about 28 miles from Quality RV door, and advertised the same brand Quality had contracted with the manufacturer and they told him they couldn't do anything about it.

As a result of hurricanes in Miami and along the east coast of Florida, Mr. Brown of FEMA contacted George, relative to travel trailers for emergency residents. He sold one to FEMA and a family from Miami called and said they were coming to see what Quality RV had. They arrived two days later, and selected one they wanted. They asked how soon they could get it, and George told them the next day. They arrived the next morning, and Quality installed their hitch and electrical hookups, and had the trailer serviced at the same time. About noon, they were ready to go, and they had a certified check for the total amount. They thanked Quality for their rapid response and returned to Miami. Incidentally, Mr. Brown would eventually became the Director of FEMA.

The Pensacola dealer had gone to Miami, as many dealers did, and set up a lot there. They were there two days, until the City told them to get out of the area, because they were not welcome and did not have a permit, and refused to purchase one. The dealer could do nothing but return to Panama City.

In January 1994, the Pensacola dealer purchased the former Dothan Camper Sales, and started advertising and selling the same units as Quality from that lot, which was in the same town and eight miles from the Quality RV door. Again, the manufacturer denied this although they had proof of it. Incidentally, no representative of the manufacturer ever visited Quality RV lot after the first visit by their former President, David, just before they started selling the brand.

Quality RV had a new travel trailer sold to a local customer. It was in the shop to be serviced, and a storm erupted. A tarp used to cover one end of the shop became loose, and whipped the trailer with a large metal bolt attached to the tarp. One side was damaged and a window was broken. George ordered the metal for the side and the window. They were delivered two days later when the manufacturer had a new trailer going south.

The repair was almost finished, when the customer arrived to check on the trailer. They asked what had happened, and the service manager told them the truth. All employees had been instructed to never lie to a customer and not to try to "pull the wool over their eyes." They requested Quality to order them another trailer, and Quality got them a replacement in about one week. In June, George Kathryn and both their sons met at Dolly Wood, TN. They had cabins for each family at Hidden Valley Resort. They spent one day in Dolly wood and saw several shows. They also toured Pigeon Forge, Sevierville and Gatlinburg, TN.

A couple was going from South Florida to their home in the Midwest, when they stopped at the Alabama Rest Stop, just inside Alabama near the Florida line. While walking around the Motor Home, the man dropped dead from a massive heart attack. The wife had it towed to the Catholic Church in Dothan, and the Catholic Father called George to appraise it. He spent about 2 hours on the appraisal, and the Father asked him what he would offer for it in cash. George left him the bid, and returned to the lot. About 10 days later the couple's two grown sons stopped at the lot to thank them for our assistance. They had decided to keep the Motor Home, and return to the couple's home in Florida. They were told that the Motor Home needed to be serviced and checked prior to their trip to Florida. They declined, knowing very little about the Motor Home, and did not think it needed servicing. George told them fine, and wished them good luck. The next day, the Service manager received a call from the sons, and they told him they wished they had listened to Quality RV. They got to Northern Florida, the engine ran out of oil, and that ruined the engine.

1994 was a year of strife, both within and outside. The other dealer continued to openly advertise the same brand at prices below Quality RV cost. Quality RV had hired a Salesman from Florida, who thought he was the best. He was named Sales Manager, on the understanding that he could train and urge others to be better salesmen. He started by firing a good friend of George, which was a good salesman, just because he just didn't like him. His personal life was a shambles. Drinking heavily and taking up with women he met at a local nightclub. He moved in with one in Georgia for a few days, until he caught her smoking marijuana on one morning. He had brought her to the office, holding hands and talking. His wife was still in Florida, and he couldn't seem to make enough money for his family and escapades. He would frequently find some excuse to go to town with the company truck. It was found out that he went to the other dealer just to "chat". He was a con artist, and would periodically go to Kathryn's desk and persuade her to write him a check for advance, without the manager's knowledge. He and Kathryn would leave for lunch within five minutes of each other, and return within five minutes of each other, whether it was 30 minutes or two hours. It could never be found out where either of them was going to lunch. George didn't suspect any misconduct, but the rest of the employees each individually came to him and asked him if he had noticed this pattern, and told him that something was going on. This lowered the morale of the employees. He could tell that one did not understand business, and was getting stressed out with unpaid bills accumulating. The Parts manager was frequently told not to order any parts. George had been approving all parts orders for some time. The parts and service had been steadily increasing to over $250,000 per year, and it began dropping because the Parts and Service managers could not order parts and supplies for their customers.

One individual came to George one afternoon, and told him he had won the Florida Lottery, and wanted to buy the longest best fifth wheel travel trailer, a good brand, with all the extras he could get. George knew he had won, because he had seen the notice at the Lottery store. George found a Prowler, and figured the cost of it. He told George that he expected him to make a good profit. When he came to the bottom line, he wrote a deposit to Quality RV for $5000.00. He complimented George for giving him the attention he did. He told George that he was going to buy a one-ton dually to pull the trailer with. He went to the Ford dealer in Dothan, but no one would talk to him because he was dressed in work clothes. He went to Enterprise, and they located him the truck he wanted. He brought it to Quality RV to install the Fifth Wheel hitch, which was a special order because of the weight carrying capacity required. When the trailer was delivered, he brought his truck, and worked with the service personnel to learn more about it. He wrote a check for the balance owed, and left. He had left his job as a truck driver when he won the lottery. The next time anyone heard of them, they had bought a trailer park in Arizona. It was sometime during the Summer, that Kathryn was singing with a group, and complained that George never taped their performance. They were staging a show at the Catholic Church, and George closed up early, went home, cleaned up, gathered his recording equipment and went to the show. When he got there, Kathryn met him at the door and told him to "get out with that damn camera. You are not going to record that show." He told her OK, and went home, and lay on the sofa to rest. When she came home, he told her that he didn't appreciate her conduct and an argument ensued because she didn't agree. George found out later that caused him a minor stroke, which left his right Diaphragm paralyzed. This would limit his breathing forever.

In September 1994, George's mother wanted transfer from her home to Gran's Home, because she had noticed she was getting unaware of whether the electric kitchen range and/or oven was turned off, and she was afraid that she would get the house afire. He entered her there, and bought a lift chair, so that she could better get up and down, because of her hip deterioration. She stayed there several months, and during that time he had to take her to the hospital for recurrence of a bleeding ulcer. She had to have a total of 14 pints of blood before the ulcer subsided. In 1994, he paid a total of $17,580.00 from Quality R.V Sales plus $2645.00 from personal account for her care. In December 1994, her health had deteriorated to the point that she had to have full time nursing care. George applied for Medicare/Medicaid and was told that she qualified for it. She had used up all the home assets, plus what he and the Corporation had given her.

On 02-21-95, he was notified that her request for Medicare/Medicaid was denied because of too many assets [more than $2000.00]. This was a lie, and reflects just how they think and the unprofessional attitude and incompetence they had. This was because her name was on the house sales Contract, although she had borrowed more than the value for medical expenses, in addition to what George and the Corporation had paid.

The last of December, George gave his oldest salesman an award for the best salesman of the year. In December 1994, Lee's personal lifestyle got the best of him, and he took off for two weeks to "rest up". He never returned to the lot, but went to work for the other dealer in Dothan. He left about $1200 in advances Kathryn had given him checks for after a "sob story."

The year 1995 was a disaster. The Pensacola dealer who had moved to Dothan kept advertising and selling the brand from their lot. In May, the manufacturer sent a letter canceling the Quality RV dealership. When questioned, they told George that they could not service and repair slide-outs in the units. This was a lie because they had been recognized for their well-equipped shop and outstanding personnel George had already talked to several Attorneys about a Suit against the manufacturer, the other dealer and the holding company. The manufacturer offered to repurchase all units they had for one year or less. This included all but one unit, which was not saleable because of water leaks and interior damage. George notified the floor plan finance company to pick up the units. The sixteen units they had for a year or less had water leaks, and they couldn't obtain material from the manufacturer for repair. The bellies were full of water when received, the trim under the refrigerator was damaged, the carpet was damaged, and the plywood flooring under the carpet was wet. They found an Attorney in Montgomery that would take the case against the manufacturer on a 100% Contingency. The floor finance company would not take any action on the manufacturer's offer. When parts orders from the manufacturer were sent to Quality RV, they demanded payment by cash and no checks, upon delivery.

They continued to operate on a reduced staff, but one employee was becoming so confused, and George advised her to reduce the time spent in the business, because she was so busy singing, with running errands to Credit Unions and Banks to deliver Loan Packages, pick up checks, making deposits in the bank, picking up supplies, etc. George removed her as a corporate shareholder, and cancelled her as Secretary of the Corporation. She became more confused and more disturbed, mainly because she could not comprehend the increased volume this business and how it had to be conducted.

George's mother was still at the Nursing home, and he continued to visit her almost every day. The Nursing Home Administrator would verbally attack both Kathryn and George for not paying the charges that Medicare/Medicaid had refused to pay, which was approximately $6400.00. George contacted the State Attorney General and the Alabama Medicaid Administrator, to no avail. Kathryn could not visit the nursing home because of this harassment.

The floor plan finance company started to charge Quality RV a higher rate of interest, and curtailment charges, in violation of their prior agreement. Quality RV was selling other brands in addition to the prime. George filed Suit against Thor, Dutchmen, and Emerald Coast R.V in May 1995. The local Bank that was financing used units, started pressuring them for curtailment charges. Comments were spreading that they were going bankrupt by a Bank employee and to their Corporate Lawyer [who was also a customer]. Word spread like wildfire to customers and potential customers all over town, and further lowered the morale among the employees.

He could tell that his employee was stressed out, partly because of out-side activities, and did and would not listen to instructions on business eth-ics and business procedures George had been educated and experienced for. He was called stupid, an idiot, crazy, and several other degrading names. A Bank employee friend was confided in, which was also a divorcee. She told him that if he pursued a divorce, he would have to provide her with the standard of living she had been used to. This Bank employee spread the comments to her fellow employees, and soon all over town. She was fired from the bank for her activities and outside comments. Divorce was out of the question, because he knew what the results would be and cost him, and George would be chastised forever. George intended to put his home life first. He had thought about redirecting the business to some other com-modity, Rental Agency, etc. The floor plan finance company would not separate the accounts among the manufacturers Prowler was the best seller, and Fleetwood would have continued with them as a dealer under phased back operations.

He experienced extreme pressure to go bankrupt and close the doors. No one would listen to him, or review the Profit and Loss Statement and Balance Sheet, which was prepared Quarterly. The Nursing Home kept harassing him for the charges for his mother that Medicaid would not pay. Customers declined because of the rumor that they were bankrupt, and the Parts manager had to tell them on several occasions that he could not order accessories and parts for them because someone had told him not to order any parts, although he had the procedure implemented that George would approve all parts orders. The secretary was doing all the clerical work, bookkeeping, and typing Loan Packages, Titles and Reports, and Kathryn came into the office to write checks. Kathryn opposed the idea of hiring a bookkeeper to keep the records he needed, because she had her procedure of Checkbook entries, and the corporation needed more depth.

She didn't like or trust any of his employees, or people he worked with. He had been accused for several years of having affairs with every female he worked with. If this were the case he would have not have achieved the status and trust among friends and associates. About the first of September 1995, George's son was called to help force him to a Bankruptcy Lawyer. George was showing a customer units they had in stock when the phone rang and he gave the price list to him to handle while George answered the phone. He returned to the customer when he got off the phone, and the son begged him to close up and meet an appointment with the Bankruptcy Attorney.

George closed up early, and they went for the appointment, but no one else appeared. George explained to his son and the Attorney that he was trapped in a box, and he could sell out, and recover. Later, Kathryn and George had an appointment with this attorney to deliver a check or $500.00 for him to start the procedure. The attorney explained the financial consequences. Incidentally, the Profit and Loss Statement as of July 1 showed a good profit, and the Balance Sheet showed a net worth of over $400,000.00. No one was interested in these statements, nor could the players interpret them. Also the general rule of thumb is that bankruptcy is not an option if a company can pay off outstanding debts in five years or less.

George's son referred George to a CPA, from Montgomery for an audit of the business. George already had an Accountant he had been using for several years. The one from Montgomery would have charged $500.00 per day, which Quality RV didn't need or could afford.

Because of the pressure from all sides, George closed the business on October 1, 1995. On October 2, he removed some important documents from the office because of the threat of a hurricane, which was approaching. He had called the Floor Plan finance company and told them that he was closing the business and to initiate action to pick up the units. On the day these units were picked up, the Fleetwood Finance Rep came in and asked what was going on. George told him what had happened, and he asked why he didn't let him know, that Quality RV could reopen and keep the Prowler units, and continue. Knowing the circumstances, George told him he had no other choice but to close the business. The Fleetwood representative called another dealer to pick up the Fleetwood units, with the understanding that George retained the option to sell any units before the pickup. George sold three units to customers he had in process.

On October 2, 1995, a Hurricane went through, and damaged some inventory, and uprooted some trees on the lot. This was not covered by insurance, as claimed by the John Deere Insurance Co. Also in this period, someone had rigged a LP gas bottle in the kitchen of the office with a candle, supposedly to start a fire in the building. The next morning, George opened the office, opened all doors and windows, and warned the technician when he arrived not to smoke until the gas was cleared out. A week later, George went to the business to get the Sunday paper, and everything seemed normal. He did not go into the gate or the office. He went to a restaurant to have breakfast, and then went to the Nursing Home to visit his mother. Shortly after he got home, his Secretary called to inform him that the office was on fire. He went immediately to the fire, and the firemen were there, along with the Deputy Sheriff. The fire had been extinguished, but he was informed he could not inspect the damage until the State Fire Marshall could investigate. About 10:30, he was allowed to go into the office. It made him sick, because they had worked hard to improve the business property. George immediately noticed that several files were missing, as well as many parts and accessories. He had a motor home in the shop, and he moved it outside away from the building.

Whoever set this fire, undoubtedly was someone that wanted them out of business, or inflicted the final blow due to the circumstances. He thought about the Ft. Rucker NCO that was scared when he saw him, the Pensacola dealer who had pressured the manufacturer to close Quality RV out, or some disgruntled employee. The most likely was the "Gypsies", or otherwise known as "Irish Travelers" who had given them trouble before, and had recently moved into the trailer park two miles up the road. However, the County Deputy Sheriff played Poker with them and would not touch them with a ten-foot pole. It will probably never be known for sure who did this.

George called John Deere Insurance Co., and they told him they would send an adjuster. They hired a local adjustment agency, and the employees started assessing the damage. George figured the damage, missing parts and supplies, and shop tools and supplies at about $120,000.00. He continued to use his van and cellular phone to conduct the business of selling out inventory, working with the adjuster, and other suppliers. The adjuster would not listen to their estimates, cut the loss, and blamed George for the fire, because the State Inspector had determined that it was set with a flammable liquid. Quality RV kept a 5-gallon can of gasoline in the shop for cleaning parts, and for the lawn mower. The Deputy confiscated the empty can, and the lock for the gate. George was in contact with the adjuster twice per week, and for some reason he was dragging his feet. George got tired of the delay, and hired an Auctioneer to sell the remaining inventory and Real Estate. He scheduled the auction for December 2, 1995. They also lost about $30,000.00 on inventory because of the forced sale.

George had been negotiating for lease of the office space and lot since the third week in September. Under the agreement, he would remain as Office Manager, and some of his employees would remain, especially those interested in the construction trades. This fire interrupted these plans, except if he could obtain an equitable insurance settlement to repair the office space, they could renew negotiations.

Someone who wanted him out of business badly apparently started the fire. The ones known that were capable and possibly had some influence were: The National Sales Manager for the manufacturer, and the "Sales Manager" from Florida, who left Quality RV to work for the other dealer. The national sales manager was looking at selling more of their brand in the area than Quality was. He was a snake in the grass and capable of anything for his benefit. The other was also an opportunist, who would do almost anything to benefit himself. The "Irish Travelers" who were always trying to steal parts and were capable of anything. What gave them the clue was who else would be interested in stealing parts and accessories, and office records and setting a fire to keep them from continuing business. Some have insinuated an inside sabotage, but no employee was considered capable of that. The only possibility was some rumors and lies that were spread around. In any case, the lies and statements by some didn't help.

After the sale the first of December, the Insurance Adjuster finally was trying to get the case closed. George had furnished him volumes of information on inventory, damage, etc. As mentioned before, he proved total loss at about $120,000, but after much arguing, the Adjustor held fast on a limit of $25,000. It is not known what the adjustor's commission was, but it was in the thousands of dollars. The John Deere Insurance Claims Adjuster told him that that was all they could afford. This was the final blow, and George decided to quit for good, because everyone seemed to be against him. He was still working out of his van on a cellular phone.

Christmas passed, and in January, a peanut vendor, approached him to purchase the property. He had saved $10,000 for a down payment, and wanted to finance the rest of the payoff. The bank would not finance him, because his business was all cash, and he could not furnish any credit history. He prepared a financial summary with an accountant, and provided it to the bank. They agreed to the transfer, but George had to co-sign for him.

After a year, Mr. Whipple told George that another friend of theirs would loan the balance due, at a lower percent interest. He agreed to pay all closing fees, so George finally got out of it. At the auction in December, it the best bid for the real estate was $74, 000, and the balance due was about $98,000. In all, George lost about $500,000 on the sellout. In eight years Rick, the peanut vendor, paid off the loan, and later turned down an offer for $250,000 for the property. George could not find any job in Dothan because the derogatory lies had been passed around hat he was crazy, stupid, a liar, etc.

In summary, he couldn't have a computer to put more than 3000 names in for direct mail. This was impossible without a computer. The derogatory comments passed to employees, customers, and associates did not help either. These derogatory comments were picked up by the other dealer and fed to the manufacturer. The statement that Quality RV was bankrupt was an outright lie. He will always think these actions precipitated the downfall. In addition, the costs to provide his mother would not be reimbursed or paid by the Medicare/Medicaid system, causing another burden on Quality RV.

As a result George has lost respect for the Recreational Vehicle and associated businesses, and will never own a Recreational Vehicle or patronize the associated companies. These include the manufacturer, the Insurance Company, the holding company, the finance companies, the other RV dealer, and one parts supplier. He also lost faith in the same Government system to which he had given 29 years of dedicated service.

CHAPTER VI

Post Retirement And Sales

George purchased a new home computer, and started a family history with notes and correspondence his mother had kept. He contacted other family members for information, and contacted many graveyards, genealogical organizations, and data generated from Family Tree Maker.

In April or May, George's younger son asked him to be on outside salesman for him, because his business was growing. George decided to do this, so he went to Gale's office and picked up catalogs, leads, and other materials to pass out to Architects and Contractors. He started out on draw against commission, and worked hard every day telephoning Architects, Parks and Recreation Departments and Contractors, and traveling every week to visit them. They were Manufacturers Agents for Playground Equipment, Site Furnishings, Glue Laminated and Heavy Timber for structures. George had a separate phone line for business calls, Fax, and Internet, which included E-Mail. He covered Shows in Georgia, Clemson, SC, Florida, and Alabama. He then changed from commission to working for expenses and some spending money.

In July 1996, George traded his Customized van for a 1996 demonstrator Ford F-150 Pickup, and purchased a camper cover for it so he could haul samples and supplies without them getting wet. The van was too tall to get into parking garages in cities like Atlanta. He stayed at the cheapest Motels, mainly Super-8; ate sandwiches for lunch and dinner, and used breakfasts provided by the Motel. He would visit up to 14 prospects daily, and send catalogues to the ones he could not visit. He would spend the morning calling Architects from the Motel to screen them for the ones he felt worthwhile. As soon as he finished the calls, he would visit the Architects he had selected, then after 5:00 PM, when most businesses were he closed, he would travel to the next Town/City. At night he would prepare packets to mail to prospects he had called that he did not have time to visit, and would mail them from a Post Office that he would pass by during travel to another City.

In about May 1996 he had noticed that someone in the Nursing Home had switched the lift chair he had bought for his mother, for a cheap recliner. He asked several personnel what had happened, but all gave him a sheepish look, and denied any knowledge of the switch. After pressuring them they came up with the story that the lift chair was broken, and their repairman scrapped it. It could have been repaired, if only they had contacted George. Their excuse was that they tried to contact him, but were unable to. This was an outright lie, because he kept the office informed of contacts for not only him, both of his sons and his brother.

The first part of 1997, George and Kathryn decided to sell their house in Dothan and move to Greenville, because they were both making many trips to Greenville for grandsons' activities, and to assist Gale. They had already located the house they could afford and wanted, which was 122 Woodland Drive, across from the Middle School in Greenville. When they got a Contract on the house in Dothan, they put a deposit on the Greenville house. The only problem, the purchasers wanted the house in Dothan as soon as possible, and the owners in Greenville could not vacate until they got their new house ready. They closed the loan in Dothan, and finalized the closing in Greenville, at the First National Bank, rented a house about a block from the house they were purchasing for three months, and the other owners paid the payment until they vacated. They moved from Dothan with a U-Haul Truck, and Gale and some of his friends helped them. It took three loads, the last being loaded by George and Kathryn.

They arrived in Greenville about Midnight thoroughly exhausted. They lived out of boxes for these three months.

In October 1997, they went to Collinsville, IL for George's 65th birthday. On October 10, they had spent the day at Dale's home, and returned to the Motel. They got a call from Dale about 11:00 PM, that the Nursing home had called and that his mother had passed away. George called the Funeral Home in Dothan, his son, Gale, and his Brother, Bob, and made necessary arrangements that night. The next day, they went to Flora to make the arrangements with Gary Bright, the funeral director. Gale picked up her belongings from the nursing home the next day, and then went to Flora. They had graveside services, and Dale also came for the services. It was raining at the gravesite, so the Undertaker provided a tent, and most attendees had umbrellas. George returned to the funeral home to finalize the final settlement, and then all returned to their homes, to resume their usual activities.

George had started paying back draws from Gale from commissions earned. Gale decided that he would rather pay all expenses plus spending money, so that George could be free to contact all Architects and Contractors on all products he offered, and perform other duties connected with the business. George started handling Trade Shows, where they had a booth. Gale went to the first one with George, and George handled the rest himself, with Gale preparing the display, and packets to distribute. George handled shows at Clemson, SC, Athens, GA, Jekyll Island Ga., Rome GA., Savannah, GA., Lake Wells, FL and Mobile, AL. He also made several trips to Atlanta, GA to visit Architects, and State/ City offices to pickup Bid Packages, Drawings, and deliver Bids.

On December 24, 1999 George had trouble breathing, and on Christmas Eve drove to the Hospital in Greenville, AL. He was put in Intensive Care section because pulse rate was extremely high. The next day he was put into a private room, with full time monitoring. He was told not to get out of bed without the assistance of a Nurse. He was on Oxygen full time, and the Cardiologist prescribed medication she thought he needed. He was diagnosed with Congestive Heart Failure and Atrial Fibrillation. He spent all week in the hospital, before he was released, on medication for these. He soon found he was over medicated, and the medications were adjusted. In February, he again had a weak feeling, and had trouble breathing. This time Kathryn took him to the hospital Emergency Room. He was kept for another week, before he could be released.

The Lawyer in the Suit against RV manufacturer, the holding company and the Pensacola dealer scheduled arbitration in February 2000. It was cancelled, because the arbitration was scheduled at the same time George was in the hospital. No depositions had been taken from anyone except George, and the President of the Pensacola RV dealer. The Arbitration was rescheduled for later, and the Lawyers had selected a retired Probate Judge from Montgomery. His fee was $500.00 per hour, and the Defense representative had no authority to finalize a settlement. The arbitrator was not worth $30.00 per hour, much less $500.00. They finally offered a settlement in November. He was forced to accept it because of the circumstances. He netted about $22,000.00, after deduction of attorney out-of-pocket expenses, which was used to pay off the most important bills from Quality RV Sales, Inc. As a result, George lost respect for Lawyers and Judges in general and the Recreational Vehicle and associated industries.

Also during this time the Nursing Home in Dothan had filed a claim against George for his mother's bills. He had hired a local attorney in Greenville to settle it. The Attorney did some good research, and determined that it was illegal to charge a third party for medical expenses. He presented the case to the Judge in Dothan, who was also a Professional Engineer, who ruled in the defendant's favor.

In March 2000, He found out that he could not urinate. The Doctor immediately determined that he must see the Urologist immediately. He went to the Urologist, and he inserted a probe, and found that George had a blocked urine tube, inserted a Catheter, which he had to wear for almost four weeks, until he could be admitted to the Hospital in Montgomery, AL for Surgery. The surgery was in the morning, and that evening the Urologist's father came into the room, to check George. The drainage was clearing up, and he told George that his son would be in about 4:00AM the next morning, to take the Catheter out. The next morning, the son, Peter came into the room about 8:30 AM, and checked the drainage. It was cleared up, and he was asked if he was going to remove the Catheter. He replied, that he would not remove it, but he would tell the nurse to remove it. That was a relief, and he told George to restrain from lifting for a month.

George had saturated his computer memory, mostly with the Family Tree data. He transferred the files to floppy discs, and deleted all the programs from the hard disc. He sold it, and bought a new computer with much more memory, under a Lease-Purchase plan.

In 1999, Gale and Phyllis decided to build their "Dream Home" on a lot in a new development. George made many trips to Montgomery to pick up materials and supplies for the new house. Gale had provided Credit Cards for Home Depot, and a Visa for other stores. He was very busy with his business and keeping the house construction on track. Phyllis had been teaching for several years in the Greenville Elementary School, was very busy teaching at Fort Dale Academy, where the Grandsons had both attended all their school years. Gale had been using a flat bed bumper mount trailer he and his office neighbor, Freddy had bought in partnership. He had many projects he needed to transport materials to, so he purchased a heavy duty Ford F-350 Diesel Dually truck. George took it to

Dothan to get the Fifth Wheel hitch and Electrical hookup installed. He had purchased a new 30 ft. Fifth Wheel Flat Bed Trailer from Trailer World in Ozark, and after the hitch was installed, George picked up the trailer on his way back to Greenville. The bumper mount trailer that Gale had with Freddy was stolen one night from their lot. They later bought another bumper mount flat bed trailer, which George took the Dually to Dothan to get a hitch installed, and again picked up the new trailer at Trailer World in Ozark. On one trip to Dothan, George was approaching Midland City, when he noticed an auto meeting him going airborne. He immediately called 911 on his cell phone, and within minutes a fire truck and ambulance were there. The auto rolled about three times, and landed upright. A fire in the auto erupted, and one passerby used a fire extinguisher and his jacket to extinguish the fire. George waited until the injured people were in the ambulance safely, and continued on his way.

George made many trips to transport materials to Calloway Gardens, GA, Charleston SC, Atlanta, GA, Destin FL, Tyndall AFB at Panama City, FL and some other locations. Gale had a very large project at Calloway Gardens, and the most trips were made there to deliver materials.

The bumper mount trailer had some drawbacks, in that the loader was inexperienced with this type of trailer, and frequently would load it too heavy on the rear, which would make the trailer sway at average speeds.

George decided he would use his research experience and work on a series of books to make the reader feel good, and relate experiences and pitfalls to be aware of. He had been researching data and finalizing his first Manuscript and found that none of the Publishers would publish it, so he revised to one, which was more lengthy and reserved and put a different slant to the idea. Minerva Press at Miami agreed to publish it for a fee. He thought it was high, and did not readily accept it. Athena Press bought Minerva, and they offered a sizable discount, so he accepted these terms.

With the cooperation of several relatives, he organized a family reunion at Flora, IL for June 2000. Since this was the first ever reunion, he met relatives had never met. They had a turnout of about 85 relatives, but his younger son and his family could not attend because of schedule conflicts.

Gale had bought a new Ford F-250 four-wheel drive pickup, because the transport of materials was increasing. Again, he sent George to Dothan to get the hitches installed.

Two playground sets to be delivered Northern Alabama. The bumper mount trailer was heavily loaded, and on I-65 in Birmingham, it began to sway, and George was lucky to accelerate and straighten it up. The set on the rear was for delivery first. After it was unloaded the towing characteristics improved, with no other problems going to the final stop.

George also made some trips to Louisiana with the F-350 Diesel and gooseneck trailer to pick up lumber from a mill.

He made several trips to project sites in Atlanta. On one occasion, they had a project in Atlanta that they were transporting material to, and Matt, one of of Gale's employees, had taken one load with the F-250 four- wheel drive and the 30 ft gooseneck trailer. The next load was with the bumper mount trailer and the F-350 Dually. The trailer was loaded heavy on the rear end, and was very unstable. George had the load adjusted after the first trial run, and on the second trial run, decided to take it to Atlanta, although 45 MPH was the maximum speed that was safe without swaying violently. At the second exit in Georgia on I-85, near LaGrange, at about 8:00 PM, George was in the left lane at the intersection to let traffic enter the interstate. It was nighttime, and he noticed a green auto coming up on the right side. When he got even with the truck, the auto was skidding sideways perpendicular to the truck. George applied the brakes to evade him, but the other driver started to skid backward, and he was hit on

George's right front corner and the auto's right front corner. When they both stopped, George called 911 on the cell phone then went to the auto to determine if anyone was hurt. Neither of them was injured, so they waited for the Trooper to arrive. The 911 operators dispatched a fire truck and ambulance, but when they found out they were not needed, they returned to their base. The Trooper interviewed both drivers. He asked George how fast he was going. George replied, "45 MPH." The Trooper said, "That truck will go faster than that, won't it?" George replied, " Yes, it will, but any faster we would have wood all over the highway." After measuring the skid marks, he asked the other man how fast he was going. He replied, "70 MPH." The trooper stated, "At 70 MPH, the skid marks would be 128 ft. Yours are 458 ft. Does that tell you something? We have information you don't have, and the skid marks you had, indicates you were going at least 100 MPH." The other driver received 4 tickets, and George had to bend the right fender away from the tire, so he could proceed to the next exit for a motel. He called Gale about what had happened, and called Matt in Atlanta to tell him where he was. It was agreed that Matt would come to the motel the next morning to discuss their next activities.

The next morning, when Matt arrived, he insisted that he would switch trucks, and take the load to Atlanta. They hooked the trailer on the F-250 four-wheel drive truck and both left the motel parking lot at the same time. George started back to Greenville with the Dually. He had gone about 15 miles when he got a call from Matt that he had a problem, and had almost had a disaster. George turned around, went back just past the intersection where he had stayed overnight, made a U-turn and pulled to the shoulder behind Matt. He had just left the intersection, and started to accelerate when the trailer started to sway, threw him out of control, and he crossed the median and stopped on the shoulder on the southbound side. He had dented the tailgate on the truck, the trailer had one broken wheel and a flat tire on the other axle, both on the right hand side, and the load had shifted.

George spent about 30 minutes calling for a tire shop or a tow truck to assist them. Finally about one and one half hours later, a tire shop sent a truck. They replaced the flat tire with a used tire removed the broken wheel. Matt eased the damaged trailer to the motel parking lot and they discussed their next action. They decided that to would transfer the load to the gooseneck trailer, and Matt would take the load to Atlanta, while George got the other trailer repaired and returned to Greenville with the F-250 Dually truck. George went to a service station nearby and inquired about someone to help transfer the load. One man volunteered to assist, and he helped Matt transfer the load. When the damaged trailer was empty, he took it to the tire shop for repair. This was just before 5:00 PM, and they were ready to close the shop. It was agreed George would return the next morning, and he returned to the motel.

The next morning, George returned to the tire shop, and was told that they had the tires needed, but he would have to get the wheel from a trailer manufacturer at the first exit in Alabama. George went to the trailer manufacturer and purchased a wheel, took it to the tire shop, and went to lunch. After lunch, they replaced the wheel and two tires, and he returned to Greenville. He took the truck to a body shop and got an estimate in the truck, assembled costs involved, and forwarded it to the other drivers Insurance Co. It was about 3 days later before he could get the accident report from the GA Trooper office in LaGrange, GA.

Gale and family moved into their new house in the fall of 1999, and had a great Christmas, the first in their new home.

In January 2000 Kathryn and George spent a weekend at the Grand Hotel in Point Clear on Mobile bay courtesy of Gale for a Christmas gift This was very relaxing and an enjoyable vacation.

Gale had a large construction project at Charlotte, NC. George made several trips there to deliver supplies and materials. Later, he had one at Charleston, SC, to which he also made several deliveries.

As mentioned before, the first Family Reunion was held at Flora, IL in June and they had a very good turnout. 2000 was a busy year. George sold the house on Woodland Drive, partly because they couldn't afford some of the needed improvements and the three levels it was becoming more difficult for them to climb the steps. They had installed a new roof, put sod on some bare spots in the yard, and planted many shrubs and flowers Also, they had to have the air conditioner repaired, and modified the kitchen for the large double-door refrigerator and converted the kitchen broom closet to shelves for a pantry. They decided that the smaller house Gale had vacated was the ideal one for them because of its convenience and single level construction. George continued to travel to achieve more business, and run errands for the business.

In the Fall 2000, George's Urologist tried to insert a probe to check for the Prostate growth, but it would not go in without severe pain. He told George to come to Montgomery hospital for an operation to remove the obstruction. He went as an outpatient, and after the operation, he told George that he had scar tissue that had almost blocked his Urinary tube. He had slit the scar tissue, and inserted a catheter to keep it open until it healed. Again, he had to wear the Catheter for four weeks, before the Urologist would remove it. Afterward, everything was fine, with no other problems in that area.

In November 2000, George had heard about County Tax Sales, and had some funds to invest. He corresponded with the Clay County, IL Tax Collector and Recorder, and attended the sale the first part of November. At the Tax Sale, he asked the County Officials what the procedure was for obtaining a Tax Deed. They told him that if the property was not redeemed, and he paid the subsequent taxes two more times, he would receive a Tax Deed. The reason he went to Clay County, IL was because he was raised in that area and knew the landscape well.

The latter part of 2000, their daughter-in-law, Phyllis was consulting doctors, and required more of Gale's time and. attention. About July, she was diagnosed with cancer. She became weaker despite the best care and the best Doctors and during the fall, but didn't want anyone to recognize it. In November, Gale and family, as well as his parents were invited to her parent's house in Geneva for Thanksgiving dinner. Everyone noticed she grew tired easily. By Christmas, she had become weaker and required pain medication. Gale moved his office computer to the house so he could continue business from there. George kept working to keep jobs coming up for him to bid. Gale's Secretary and Freddy, kept the office running. Gale's secretary continued to make all quotes on Playground equipment and site furnishings, and Gale was approving all bids, and making the bids on Glue Laminated beams and Heavy Timber projects.

The pain continually got worse for Phyllis requiring more pain medication, and she became weaker. George, and Kathryn took care of many errands. In May 2001, Phyllis passed away. Their oldest son, Dale and family went to Greenville for the services, but it was a sad day for all of them.

In June, they had the family reunion at Flora, IL, and due to the family catastrophe, Gale and family could not attend. George and Kathryn's 50th wedding anniversary celebration was at Hilton Head Island, SC at the Hilton Hotel and the Planters Inn in Charleston, SC, compliments of their sons.

The latter part of 2001 South Carolina was awarded to the Gale's territory for Structural Wood Systems, the manufacturer of wood laminated beams. The previous territory was Georgia, Northern Florida and extreme South Alabama. George started to cover South Carolina, visiting and calling

Architects and Contractors. They had a few projects outside these areas and one in North Carolina due to special circumstances. George covered each city in South Carolina from referrals from the Internet, local phone books, referrals and visiting offices that collected construction information.

In August, Gale married Jody, which George and Kathryn thought a lot of after they got to know her They moved into Gale's house, and did some remodeling to accommodate her two sons. Afterward, due to sentimental concerns, they remodeled Jody's house to accommodate 4 sons, moved to her house and sold the previous house Gale had built.

In October 2001, George participated in the tax sale in Illinois. He was told the same procedure as before. Several of the parcels were redeemed during the year, and the owner paid the stated interest.

In the latter part of 2001, George finally got Minerva Publishing Co in Miami, FL to agree to publish the first book. He chose the name Schlegel because it was the German version of his family name. A friend commented that the Publishing operation was very slow, but to hold in there. He reviewed it three times, during the year, and it was finally published in February 2003. They had been reviewing it since about February 2002. The common concept of publishing a book makes the Author an instant millionaire. This is erroneous, unless the Author is a high level prostitute, a criminal or a politician, all of National fame. The truth is that it is a very competitive process. The only way to get the book published was to pay a cooperative fee, four payments of $1160.00, for a total of $4640.00. In return, they pay 45 percent of the wholesale price until the investment is recovered, and 22 percent from there on. One of the delays was the purchase of Minerva by Athena Press, and their relocation to London.

During Easter Vacation, Dale was able to spend a few days with his parents. He really enjoyed riding the four-wheeler ATV on Gale's farm, and enjoying the company with Christopher and his parents. He preferred to spend the nights at Gale's farm in the bunkhouse that had been converted from a stable.

Meanwhile, during the reviews during 2002, George was working on a Family Heritage, which was the most complete family history ever accomplished. They had their annual Family Reunion in June 2002. Not such a good turnout as they had had before, but better than 2001. Both sons were able to attend. The early fall of 2002, George finished the Family Heritage, after about 15 years gathering and organizing the information. His mother had collected loads of information over the years, but with the help of the modern computer Word Processing, he was able to organize it. During the next few months, he distributed 30 copies of this. Also he began assembling a collection of facts, stories, tales and jokes collected over a period of about five years.

In October 2002, the business he had been working was receding. He really didn't realize how much until a talk with Gale. They both agreed that expenses to promote our products were more than he could afford. This was around George's seventieth birthday and it was time for him to pay more attention to family life, hobbies and odd jobs he had been deferring.

The time had expired for the Tax Deeds to be redeemed in Illinois. When George inquired about them, he was told that he would have to consult a Lawyer. When George consulted a Lawyer, who he had worked with for many years, he told him he had already missed one step in the process, and he sent George the Illinois Statute covering the subject. In essence, he told George that there was nothing he could do. George then filed Liens with the Clay County Recorder on the property. He then located heirs of three properties, and gave them the choice of paying the taxes, penalties and interest, or signing a Mineral Deed to George and he would pay the delinquent taxes, interest and penalties. Some decided to sell the Mineral rights to George rather than pay the liens. George made one trip to Akron OH, to finalize purchase of the deeds on two properties. He closed the other through correspondence with heirs in Texas and California. Thus, this was nothing new. George has had the reputation of accomplishing tasks that no known others could.

George continued work on the Manuscript on "Chico's Collection of Facts, Stories, Tales and Jokes. He used the same name, Herr Schlegel as the Author. It contained over 80,000 words, about 300 pages and over 300 entries. It was accepted by Athena Press, but had other contacts to negotiate with before signing a contract. The one he finally settled on, Publish America, required no cooperative payment, but the commission is significantly lower. Under this plan, He gets eight percent of the first 2,000 copies sold, ten percent on the next 8,000 copies, and 12.5 percent in excess of 10,000 copies. Under this agreement, he got 2 copies free. Under the plan with Minerva, he received 50 copies free. Only time will tell how the two plans compare.

In April 1993, Kathryn took the leadership of the local TOPS [Take off Pounds Sensibly] Chapter. She had been a member for over 20 years, and had never taken any office in the organization. Her leadership lasted two years.

In September 2003, George finished the manuscript of third manuscript on Jokes. This manuscript was sent to an agent for marketing. The next two subjects he is working on are a Biography, and one about inspirations.

In September 2004 Hurricane "IVAN" went through Alabama, following Interstate 65. As a result Greenville was hit by the northeast quadrant of the hurricane, experiencing winds of 85 MPH and gusting to 95 MPH. There were over 7000 trees down in the town of 7000 residents. Many residents experienced damage, some having to evacuate their homes until repairs could be accomplished. George was fortunate to have one tree to hit their living room, and the power was out for only four hours. He had ridden out three hurricanes, and this was by far the worst. This was the first experience he had with FEMA. Their grants are for only the poorest that cannot get loans anywhere. They were contracted by the City to remove debris, but it had to be placed on the road Right Of Way. They task the Small Business Administration to make the loans. Being retired, George didn't want any more loans. He needed help to remove some downed trees and limbs from the property. Insurance only covered the damage caused from trees striking a structure. The others were not covered. Consequently, several trees will not be removed until George can afford it.

Many of the local carpenters and tree service people ripped off the victims and insurance companies. Carpenters charged $1000.00 per person per 9-hour day labor. Tree cutters charged $700.00 for removing a tree from the house structure and removing the debris, using 4 men for 30 minutes. Some carpenters and tree trimmers who were from out of town charged much more because people affected had to get repairs as soon as possible. A year later, many repairs and debris removal have not been completed. It is estimated that it will take another 2 years to finish.

On August 29, 2005, the United States suffered the worst disaster in history. Hurricane Katrina started as a Category I when it went over the south tip of Florida. After emerging into the Gulf of Mexico, it grew into a Category 4/5 and made direct hit on the Gulf Coast near New Orleans and creating waves of 27 to 29 feet, destroying most structures and massive flooding in New Orleans. Katrina affected about 92,000 miles of area and approximately one million people were displaced. New Orleans was the hardest hit because it is in a "bathtub" with levees to protect it. It is below sea level and all water must be pumped out. To complicate the situation, levees protecting the city from Lake Pontchartrain to the North suffered breaks and dumped more water into the City of New Orleans. The pumping system was designed to handle a two-inch rain, was not maintained properly, and was grossly overloaded by the deluge of hurricane rain.

Also, it was reported that New Orleans had been sinking and the levees were sinking. The entire Gulf Coast was affected eastward as far as Destin, Florida, and northward in Mississippi to the northern one-third of the state. Tornadoes spawned by the hurricane and heavy precipitation resulted in damage in Georgia and into the Northeastern area of the United States. It was estimated that 150 miles of the coastline was destroyed and 1,400,000 people were displaced.

Some think that the Government was too slow to act. This was the most monumental task ever attempted. Any that has worked for any level of Government can understand that the Government bureaucracy is so huge, and it is relatively slow to react. For example, portable toilets were delivered on September 4, 2005, after most of the refugees were rescued. However, it was a great asset to the thousands of rescue personnel on site for an estimated two months.

Rescue of residents of New Orleans was a monumental task. Rescue personnel went house-to-house searching for survivors, and after almost a week of being without food, electricity, water, and many with flooded homes, some still hesitated to be rescued. This was mainly because they had experienced flooding before and the water soon subsided. They had a hard time realizing that it would be months before the city would be inhabitable.

One of the drawbacks was the price of gasoline and diesel fuel. Some refineries were damaged, and pipelines were affected, causing a shortage of fuel. This was unfortunate, but prices of fuel skyrocketed, causing hardship on many. Prices for unleaded regular gasoline were reported to go to $3.00 to more than $6.00 per gallon. This directly affected the tremendous cost of rescue, recovery, and distribution of evacuees; and the costs of connecting utilities and emergency repairs by government agencies and volunteers. The problem was that many companies and some investors that undoubtedly made huge profits from the circumstances. In any casualty, there are several who inflate prices at the expense of consumers and this will probably never be eliminated. The Congress and Senate don't dare to take any action at the expense of votes and financial support.

Most do not realize how much effort goes into organizing a rescue effort the magnitude of that size. This was the largest effort ever organized. Also, FEMA, the National Guard and many others just don't go into an area, until the Mayor, Governor or any other official asks them. This was part of the delay. FEMA received conflicting reports on the extent of the damage. Most intelligent people think this was the fastest response possible under the circumstances encountered.

Most news media blamed the President for the slow response. The fact was, the Hurricane Center called the Louisiana Governor and the Mayor of New Orleans and was warned on Thursday before the hurricane hit on Monday. The President and the Director of FEMA met on Friday to plan for the impact. The Louisiana Governor and the New Orleans Mayor and warned them to evacuate the City in preparation for it. It was the responsibility of the Mayor and the Louisiana Governor to take the necessary action, and ask for Federal assistance when they deemed it necessary. This was not done until Tuesday, after the levees broke and flooding was in progress. Had the Mayor and Louisiana Governor taken the necessary action, the evacuation would have been more effective. Mr. Brown, the Director of FEMA did a commendable job of organizing the evacuation of residents, and the criticism he received was uncalled for. The real reason he was relieved from on-site management was so he could attend to his duties as Director, and let the Coast Guard take over for rescue and finishing the tasks he had organized the effort. A Military Commander can muster more military support for the rescue effort, although the Coast Guard is under the Treasury Department during peacetime and under the Navy in time of war. The FEMA is charged with coordinating the first response. The problem was, FEMA could not persuade the Louisiana Governor to cooperate. The Governor is the only one that can order the National Guard, because the Governor is the overall Commander of the National Guard. This was not done, and consequently the problem was with the Governor and the Mayor of New Orleans, and not with FEMA.

CHAPTER VII

Summary

George had an extremely interesting lifetime. As a very young chap, he dreamed of airplanes and technical things. He built and flew model airplanes, drove every vehicle, including cars, trucks and farm tractors from the time he was 8 or 9 years old. During World War II, he corresponded with aircraft manufacturers for pictures of airplanes and any other information they could provide. A lady at Consolidated-Vultee Aircraft Company in Miami, Florida, named Mrs. R. Swann sent him many airplane pictures, magazines and all technical information she could. He was so thrilled with what she sent him that he told her that he wanted to be an Aerospace Engineer sometime.

By the time he was 12 years old, he became known throughout the community as an expert with mechanical things, and could fix about anything and drive anything, and could operate any equipment. When he graduated from Grade school, his father took him to Champaign, to the University of Illinois, to discuss Engineering with a Professor of Mechanical Engineering that had been a schoolmate with his father. During High School, he took all the Math and science he could get as the Professor advised. He also took Physics, Chemistry, and Shop.

He farmed with his father after he graduated from High School in 1950. . He tried to get a job at factories in the local area, but he was draft age and single, and no one would hire him. He continued farming with his father, and in 1951 decided he was ready to get married, and married Kathryn on June 17, 1951. In the fall, they went on vacation to New Orleans and Tampa Florida to visit Kathryn's aunt and his relatives around Tampa,

Florida. When he returned, the Draft Board secretary, Betty McCarthy had left a message for him to contact her immediately.

He had talked to the Navy Recruiter, and when he went to the Draft Board she showed him the letter that she had delayed sending. The Navy Recruiter was there, and asked him if he was ready to enlist. He replied yes because he didn't wish to be drafted into the Army. The recruiter prepared the paper work, and told him to be at the train station the next morning at 4:30 AM to go to St Louis to be processed.

At the end of Boot Camp, the assignments were posted. The Navy told him he had a high Mechanical and Mathematical ability, and assigned him to Aviation School at Norman, Oklahoma, and promoted to Airman Apprentice. He was elated, and this would change his life and career forever. He never dreamed he would reach the levels of professional and social activities that he experienced.

He loved aviation, and did well in the Aviation School. At the end, he was assigned to HS-3 at Elizabeth City North Carolina. This was a helicopter Anti Submarine Squadron. He really enjoyed this assignment, and was soon assigned to the tool room. He was later promoted to AD-3, and assigned as a Plane Captain for a HO4S crew. He was deployed with his crew on two Carrier cruises. He went through Air crewman training, and received extra flight pay for flying at least 4 hours per month. He was later assigned to HTU-1 at Ellyson Field, Pensacola, Florida, where he continued as an air crewman on student solo flights. When discharged in February 1956, he joined the Navy Reserve at St. Louis, which was a transport squadron. He had been promoted to AD-2 at Pensacola, and in St Louis was promoted to ADR-1. This designation was Aviation Machinist for Reciprocating Engines. He flew as Flight Engineer and dearly loved it. Later the squadron was disbanded, and they went to Chicago to another Transport Squadron. Later, the Reserve Center at Memphis, wanted them in a Patrol Squadron, and offered to pick them up on Friday night and return on Sunday evening. At Memphis, he flew as Flight Engineer, Radar Operator, Mad/Sonobuoy operator, Bombardier, and a couple of gunnery positions.

After a year back at the farm he decided to get into the aircraft industry. He entered Parks College of St Louis University in Cahokia, Illinois, which then was the best aviation college in the USA, in Aerospace Engineering. He spent three Trimesters there and ran out of money, although he was receiving Veterans Administration payments. He went back to the farm for a year then back at St Louis to work a few months at the Brown Shoe Co. Chemical plant in St Louis, and then was hired by McDonnell Aircraft Co in St Louis as a Flight Test Engineering Technical Report Writer. After several months there, he was hired in Civil Service at the Army Aviation Command in St Louis, as a GS-7 Technical writer. He spent 15 years there, in positions in Logistics, Maintenance and Project Management, and received promotions through the ranks to GS-14. He became known throughout the government and industry that he was an "Ass Kicker" and an expeditor. In other words, he knew how to get things done. He had been trained in computers, and became proficient in programming and use of output. Everything was by punch cards, and they had many personnel were involved in punching cards for input.

While there, he attended night college classes, and then a couple of good friends at the office persuaded him to finish his Engineering degree. He rearranged his working hours, and attended courses at Parks. He received several other credits that Parks would accept, scheduled two or three classes in sequence and received his BS degree in Aircraft Maintenance Engineering. After that he enrolled in the University Of Oklahoma in Foreign Relations where he earned 17 Semester hours. Then Webster University began offering MBA degree classes on site. He finished his MBA in 1976, with Majors in both Business and Foreign Relations.

While in that area, he was Assistant District Director for the Boy Scouts of America, and an officer In the Southern Illinois Citizens League, which was organized to resist the St. Louis City Earnings Tax. He farmed in Clay Co., Illinois, started Belle Valley Chemical Co, to sell janitorial supplies, bought and sold used cars and trucks, and became a Real Estate Broker.

He had several opportunities to go to Washington, DC for promotions, but declined due to the high cost of living, conditions in that area and family considerations.

He spent the last 10 years in Federal Service as a Technical Advisor to the Aviation Board at Ft Rucker, Alabama. Again, he had several opportunities to go to Washington, DC for promotions, but declined. The living costs in Alabama were significantly lower than St. Louis or Washington. At Ft. Rucker, where the Military dominance was much greater, he soon noticed that the professionalism level was significantly lower. The civilian employees were very good at their jobs, but the military dominance and attitudes of civilians degraded the overall mission performance level. He joined the VFW in Daleville, Alabama, and became a life member. He was also active in the American Helicopter Society, Army Aviation Association, Flight Frontiers Association, Elks, American Legion, and Society of Professional Engineers.

He retired on disability in 1986, and organized the Dothan Nut Company. This did not prove to be profitable due the lack of help available. In 1987, He organized Quality RV Sales, Inc. at Dothan, Alabama. The first 3 or 4 years were fun, and related business people were good. After the World War II and Korean era veterans retired, the younger replacements did not have the ethics, professionalism, etc. as their predecessors. In 1995, He got out of it by the skin of his teeth, and the aftermath was worse than anything else. This experience made some know that he was nobody to cross.

He then started selling for his son of Greenville, Alabama In this he enjoyed every minute of traveling and meeting Architects and Contractors in Alabama, Georgia, Florida, South Carolina and parts of Tennessee and North Carolina; and putting on shows for their products.

He thoroughly enjoyed the opportunity to serve his Country and Community, as well as the many professional, social, fraternal, Veterans, Boy Scouts and Civic organizations. He feels he served them well with dignity and dedication. He reached the levels and participated in things and organizations that he never thought possible when he was a child. When he was young he dreamed of being involved in Aviation because he loved aviation since he was very young building and flying model airplanes, and dreamed of being an Aerospace Engineer. He accomplished all of these and more.

During the past 50 years or more, he has made many friends, hundreds and maybe thousands, all over the world. He highly respects all of the relatives and friends he has met, regardless of their education, profession or stature, or political level. Every one of them has contributed greatly to our country and society in each of his/her own way. Due to his and other engineers and scientists, the number and casualty rates have been drastically reduced. In World War II there were about 450,000 Military lives lost in four years; In Korea there were about 55,000 lives lost in 3 years. In Viet Nam there were 58,000 lives lost in 10 years. In the past two years there have been about 1800 lives lost. The reduction in casualties can be attributed to the leadership and dedication of George and hundreds of DOD engineers and scientists, the innovative service members as well as those employed by Government contractors. It should be noted that Lawyers, Accountants, Bankers, and other non-engineers and scientists never invented anything, and the engineers and scientists have been behind the increase in technology since World II. He says he is proud of what he has done or has caused to be done for the Military, and our Society and the communities he has lived in. Of course he says there some that will not give him the time of day, but that is okay. Some may be due to envy or jealousy. He can do without them. The majority of people highly respect him and he highly respects them. An old Toast "Here's to those that wish us well, and all of those who don't can go to hell" holds truer than many realize. Now that he is past 70 years old, he will leave it to the succeeding generations to carry on, hopefully in the same or better tradition than our generation has. During the past few years his health has been deteriorating, and his energy is waning. He plans to continue the publications planned, and then hopefully pay some debts and do some traveling from the proceeds of those publications.

He has been researching many subjects most of his lifetime, the main being in improvements to Military equipment. He has written several papers on various subjects. He has always been acutely interested in improving his community and local welfare. As he says, "Since I am trained and experienced in research. I will probably continue researching some subjects until my death."

There have been many changes over the years. Many have been good, and some have been detrimental. We must be tolerant and enjoy the good things, because everything will get more complicated and worse in some cases. We must overlook the evil parts of our world society, because we cannot correct them. We must choose and trust the people we elect to represent us, because it is out of our control. Every one, as they grow up and mature has events, which may be experienced, are heard or seen, have and should not be related to anyone or in any publication.

We live in a world economy today, whereas in the past we were an isolationist society. This may be difficult for some to cope with, but they must become adjusted to the world today because we cannot and will not go backward.

His sons and now his grandsons are following the family traditions by obtaining the education and training to achieve even greater heights than the previous generations. One grandson is a Medical Doctor, another is an accountant, another has graduated from the Auburn School of Architecture, is working on a MS in Building Science and one of the few that has been a video- recorder for the Auburn Tigers football games.

He has achieved the reputation as an expert in many areas, and has influenced many to achieve success. Some of those who have chosen to not use his influence or guidance, or have crossed him have faltered, and they have suffered hardship and losses as a result. The following are recommendations, based on his experience and education:

Never let credit cards get to the point that they cannot be paid off at the end of the month. If this happens, we should stop charging and adjust to live within our means. Looking back, he has been bogged down in credit cards, and he didn't realize it until later, and he took action to get the charging stopped and the credit cards paid off.

Those starting a business should select a product or service that is a necessity. Those in the luxury categories, are subject to demand, lows and highs affected by environmental factors such as interest rates and cost of borrowing, gasoline prices, cost of living variations, and other factors.

Young people should begin college or trade school immediately after high school. They are fresh to studying, and their lifetime earning power will be greatly increased. If they prefer or have to go into military service after high school, they should get all the education available either on Base or off Base, at a local college or trade school, or by correspondence.

If you are in business or sales, and the vendor you represent changes management and policy, consider changing to another vendor.

Those preferring Military Service should get their education first, whether it is college or trade school. Thus, chances of advancement and further training will be enhanced. There are many benefits of military service, and everyone should take advantage of them.

Educational opportunities abound everywhere. Every student can find some way to attend college or trade school.

In business, there must be only one boss to make the decisions, right or wrong. Stay flexible. Always search for other, and maybe better, opportunities.

If you work for someone, be loyal to that owner, company or boss. The main things most employers look for is honesty, loyalty and dependability.

Always be on the lookout for theft or mismanagement of resources. In this day, it is difficult to hire anyone who is honest and keeps the integrity you must have in whatever you do.

Always be loyal to your employer. If in a Corporation, remember you are working for the shareholder and you are there at the pleasure of the Board and stockholders.

If you work for any level of Government, remember that you represent the taxpayer. Always remember you are also a taxpayer too, and judgments should be based honesty, integrity, and good judgment.

Always remember that any infractions on you part, will be dealt with severely, and could possibly ruin your career and reputation forever.

The wage earner must always know where his/her resources and expenditures are going, and control the expenditures and investments.

Keep your credit history clean. Remember that any derogatory entries can ruin your credit availability and result in higher interest rates for credit.

Don't rely solely on Social Security for your retirement. Start a savings plan and/or investment at a young age, which can provide the income you desire for retirement. To maintain an average standard of living, it is estimated that if you retired 10 years ago, you need retirement benefits and investments of about $1,000,000.00. Today, the amount is about 1.5 million, and the college graduates today should plan on having $2,000,000.00 or more in retirement benefits and investments and savings. No one except the poor can depend on Social Security alone to retire on, and many can supplement Social Security with a savings or investment plan that can provide a better retirement.

Plan on being ready to retire when you approach the age of 55. Some employers like older workers, but many consider people at 55 are either over qualified, ancient, senile, inadequate, etc. Some employers will root out workers at or over 55, because they can hire younger workers cheaper.

One of the best investments is a home. Plan to have it paid off as well as all credit completely before retirement.

If you need to hire a tradesman [electrician, carpenter, lawyer, etc.], do so by referral only. Some times the cheapest may be the most expensive in the long run. There are many "scam artists" that you should be aware of, and not be another victim.

Always obey the laws. Nowadays, many consider violating the laws the same as adultery, stealing, lying, etc. Participate in Veterans organizations if you are a veteran. If not a veteran, many organizations need volunteers, such as church/synagogue, hospitals, Scouts, Elks, Masons, Shriners, professional organizations and many local civic, service or fraternal organization.

Everyone should own a paper shredder. In this day, every one should shred everything that has any identifying information on it. The fraud and identification theft is increasing, and this is a reasonable way to deter that.

Never put anything in the trash that has your SSAN, bank account number, credit card numbers, drivers license number, or any other identifying number.

And the one main thing to remember is that life is short, and we only get one chance at it. We all must make the best of what we do and have while we are here.

The main attribute that he feels as important is the ability to learn as much or more than anyone else about every task, job, business, or charitable organization we delve into.

APPENDIX A

New Concepts of Maintenance Management

NOTE: The following is a Technical Paper prepared by George for graduation from the Army Logistics Course on February 17, 1967. Some of the concepts are still applicable today as predicted in the paper in the Department of Defense and are also applicable to Industry.

INTRODUCTION

Maintenance consumes approximately 25 percent of our Defense budget. This maintenance also costs approximately10 percent of all our equipment assets. It is only logical that we must constantly focus our thoughts on improved methods and practices, both in programming maintenance actions and developing new concepts to be used. These concepts must make use of all our data sources and computer programs available. Several recent advancements in this field will ultimately result in significant change sin the entire logistics management concept. High- speed computers and automated processes will allow these concepts to be realized. Sophisticated systems and equipment presently in production require a high degree of management to fulfill their assigned missions. The period is rapidly approaching when requirements personnel will utilize usage rates, mean times between failure, reliability factors, maintainability factors and failure rates to forecast requirements. These new concepts will reduce fluctuations in inventory and constant revisions to procurement, overhaul and repair of equipment. They will also tend to stabilize production schedules and allow further automation and improvement in production processes.

It is considered, due to the portion of our budget applied to maintenance, and the requirements of and assistance to the future manager, that elements discussed in the following paragraphs will greatly enhance logistics management as they become operational. The changes are on the way. It's up to the present manager to adapt himself and his operations to future resources of management.

DATA SYSTEMS AND APPLICATION.

Improvement in any type of management would be much more difficult without the aid of computer systems. Maintenance management is one phase, which is gaining rapidly in the application of these systems.

Production management, concept, theory and technique development subsequent to World War II produced new mathematical and computational requirements. These will be discussed later in Production Planning and Control.

The high speed of processing data by computers has made way for new systems such as MEADS [Maintenance Engineering Analysis and Data System], TAERS [The Army Equipment Record System], NAPALM [National ADP program for AMC Logistics Management], The Navy "3M" system, and the Air Force "66-1" system all pave the way for newer concepts of the maintenance management function. Sophisticated programs for output products, high-speed processing, huge memory units and new applications of ADP equipment are valuable assets to the manager. The use of computer analyses of tremendous volumes of data facilitates rapid reporting of performance, requirements, forecasting of trends and problem solving. Actions can be affected on possible trouble areas before the deficiency actually comes to light, thereby reducing costs and loss of mission effectiveness.

The manager must know what to do with vast amounts of data and records available to him. The analysis function must made aware of management's desires and needs, so that computers can be programmed accordingly. The effective maintenance manager is constantly searching for additional benefits, besides striving to make maximum use of these "tools" he has or soon will become available.

Increased equipment reliability, state of operational readiness, training and maintenance deficiencies, manpower requirements and future maintenance requirements are just a few of these applications for these data.

MAINTAINABILITY AND RELIABILITY.

Maintainability and reliability factors can be developed during the development of new equipment. The MEADS, thereby eliminating problems during research and development, which would otherwise require costly correction in the operational stage, will accomplish this. TAERS is the Army system, which follows on from first operation until obsolescence and disposal. Constant improvements can be made to the maintainability and reliability aspects, which were not detected during MEADS.

The theory of probability is utilized during development stages to forecast availability, probability of survival, mean time to failure, duration of downtime, maintenance man-hours and cost factors, failure rates and repair rates.

The evaluation of a system after production in field operation will be accomplished through TAERS. We can evaluate the system utilizing feedback data to verify its expected performance. Reliability, maintainability and other factors obtained are then compared with those from mathematical models. If discrepancies are found, mathematical prediction techniques must be refined and corrective actions taken to alleviate problems with the equipment.

LIFE CYCLE

The life cycle of equipment is also becoming more important. The new concept of life cycle costing is presently being developed. Thus, equipment can be programmed throughout its life cycle for economics of overhaul/rebuild versus disposal, and advance costing of every action until final disposal. The consideration of these costs is to be applied to procurement, as a prime consideration in selection of contractors.

The total cost for an item of equipment throughout its life cycle may be as much as 250 or 300 times the purchase price. This is why present procurement practices of selecting the lowest responsible bid will give way to evaluation and procurement of items with lowest cost expected during the entire life cycle.

Design, testing, procurement and all types of maintenance and cost of disposal are just a few of those costs considered in life cycle costing procedures. Reliability and maintainability factors are also used in calculating these costs. Cost differentials in technical data requirements are also significant. For example, an item with other costs equal may require development of new drawings and manuals, while a competitive item may have drawings and manuals available, which may or may not require only minor changes.

It should be noted that all items do not lend themselves to life cycle costing. Sole source type items, specification controlled items with applications controlled by the end item manufacturer, and low cost expendable items are a few of the exceptions. However, when computer programs are developed, these costs can be established for all items, including common hardware.

PRODUCTION PLANNING AND CONTROL

Critical Path Scheduling [CPS] is an application of PERT [Program Evaluation and Review Technique] has been such an effective tool for large construction and manufacturing operations that it can easily be applied to maintenance production planning, control and evaluation. This technique was initiated by the Navy in development of the Polaris system and was so successful in saving time and costs that it is being applied to almost every other type of operation. It graphically reflects the interrelationship of a variety of activities. It indicates which operations are most important, which should be given more attention and the sequence that controls overall time and/or costs. CPS is just as effective for use on jobs with 15 or 20 operations as in a project with 500 or more operations. However, as the number of operations increases, computer assistance grows more important and time saving. Generally, operations with more than 25 operations should be computerized. Simply punching a new card and re-running the whole program may make changes or revisions. The average computer of today [Second Generation] can run the entire program in less than one minute. The new "Third Generation" will be capable of running the same programs much faster.

Computer use in such areas of the maintenance budget, work order procedures, labor productivity, labor standards, measurement and appraisal of performance greatly simplify production and control.

Research and problem solving, integrating systems and control of production processes are also becoming highly automated. The application of computers for research, problem solving and simulation is already used in some organizations on a day-to-day basis.

The use of automation in machine processes is increasing rapidly. These concepts are used in all kinds of manufacturing methods now. One of the most completely automated fabrication systems is in the Cleveland Engine plant of Ford Motor Co. In this system, a combination of interconnected transfer machines takes the raw casting of an engine block and drills, mills, bores, threads, finishes and inspects with very little direct labor involved. The other processes used in repair, overhaul and preventative maintenance are rapidly becoming more automated.

Production planning and control managers must constantly be aware of new systems and procedures in order to make the maximum use of funds, facilities and personnel. They must be aware of standards and be able to detect deviations on a day-to-day basis and correct deficiencies before they develop into more serious problems.

REQUIREMENTS PLANNING

The concepts relating to maintenance management described above will result in a complete revolution in requirements planning. Requirements are presently calculated primarily on past issues and demands. This results in complete and constant changes to procurement, repair/overhaul and retirement of end items and major components. Also, computers, resulting in more efficient management, prepare supply control studies.

Future procedures will result in an even greater reduction in manpower to plan requirements and procurement actions. The factors to be used in determining requirements as mentioned in the introduction will provide management of more complex systems with a fraction of the routine review and analysis now accomplished. Computers will make automatic repair and procurement programs on major items even more manageable than presently on secondary repair parts.

The requirements planning group will become less involved in complete management of their items. The maintenance manager will contribute an increasing amount of data and responsibility used for management and materiel.

THE FUTURE

The maintenance manager of tomorrow will require more intensive training in computer and automation concepts and utilization. We are presently experiencing an evolution of business and industrial processes, organization structures and the process of managing under the impact of technological progress. This evolution is gaining speed rapidly. It threatens the survival of myopic managers and creates unlimited opportunities for those managers who fully grasp the nature of environmental changes that science is producing.

The future manager will have a remote computer control, which will portray data graphically and complete analysis of problems. He will have a voice inquiry facility and voice output from his central computer system. With these facilities, his staff will consist of a few highly trained analysts, keypunch operators, systems experts, programmers and clerks. Eventually the keypunch function will be accomplished automatically. His computer system will be such that he can "dial" any facility in the world for instantaneous reports of data. He will also be able to exchange data analysis, management decisions, graphical data, instructions and drawings with any facility in a matter of seconds. He will have hourly production reports available on demand. Any problem at any worldwide facility can be transmitted to the central computer, solved, and the answer provided to the requestor in 2 or 3 minutes, possibly half way around the world.

This manager must be thoroughly trained in every aspect. He must be an expert in maintenance, production, Automatic Data Processing and systems management. A thorough knowledge of resource management will also be a must. The computer will prepare his correspondence and reports after transmittal by voice. It should be realized at this point, that only correspondence and reports required will be those that must be documented. All data will be transmitted. All data will be transmitted at the speed of light [186,000 miles per second].

These ideas may seem too exotic, but we are in the infancy of automated management. If the manager of today wants to progress and remain a manager for tomorrow, he had better continue his thinking and training for these future concepts. Otherwise, he will be dropped to the wayside in the rapid advancement of technology.

The Probable Effect Of The Chinese Proleterian Cultural Revolution On Government Structure As Represented By The Peking Foreign Language Press.

BACKGROUND

Recent developments in Foreign Relations with Communist China, and their emergence into world prominence demand a closer look at internal actions and changes resulting in their present status. They have tremendous human resources, and if fully developed, could result in them becoming a third world "Super Power". They are rapidly increasing their agricultural and industrial output; they presently have nuclear capability; weapon technology has been rapidly increasing; education level is being improved; and population control has been implemented. The other people of the world must recognize these and other factors before present government actions can be understood and international relations can be continually improved. The Chinese thinking can be reflected only by analysis of official press releases.

The People's Republic of China has approximately 800 to 850 million, making it the most populous area in the world. There are at least 216 persons per square mile, although the distribution is very uneven. It is the second largest country of the world with 90 percent of the people living on one-sixth of the land. Two-thirds of China's area is mountainous or semi-desert, while only about one-tenth is cultivated. The population is primarily in the fertile plains and deltas of the east. One of every four persons on earth lives in China, with peasants constituting four-fifths of this population. There are more peasants than there are whites in America and Western Europe.

China is the oldest living nation in the World, and her people have the longest story of all in the human family. In the past, these people taught the rest of the World many things, some so long ago that we have forgotten how they came to us. The Chinese have probably invented and originated more than any other people with whose history we are familiar. The civilization of China is her own, while others such as the United States are only new editions revised and corrected from former civilizations. For example, the art of printing was invented in China in 932 A.D. Prior to 800 A.D., tea was discovered in Southern China as a beverage. It's early applications also included a cold plaster for rheumatism, and is used today for making ice cream in Japan.

China's proud heritage was marred by wars, famines and extreme poverty. The apparent goal of Mao Tse-tung was to improve the social structure and rebuild what had been degraded during several generations.

The Manchu dynasty, on which Chinese culture was established in modern times, ruled from 1644 to 1912. China was without effective central government for twelve years until 1925, when Chiang Kai-Shek gained control. Communist ideology was attempted in 1923, when Sun Yat-sen accepted Russian advisor Michael Borodin as his political advisor in setting up his Nationalist government and Army. China and Russia severed relations and Soviet advisors were deported in 1927, but Communist influence remained. In 1931 Mao Tse-tung was named chairman of a Chinese Soviet Republic, which gained power until 1946. Full-scale civil war in 1946 and 1947 resulted in Mao gaining control of Mainland China in 1949.

COMMUNES AND THE GREAT LEAP FORWARD

Communist Chinese economic policies have had two primary objectives: agricultural modernization and industrial development. The regime's attempt at agricultural reform and the transformation of peasants into modern producers underwent three stages of development: co-operativization [land reform, mutual =-aid teams, and "lower" co-cooperatives], Collectivization ["higher " co-operatives], and communization.

Land reform was accomplished through the Agrarian Reform Law of June 1950, which in less than two years revolutionized social relationships in the countryside by eliminating the feudal aristocracy and redistributing the land among the peasants. The land reform program was accompanied by the creation of mutual-aid teams that pooled their land, labor and farm implements. This was a step toward eventual collectivization of agriculture but the CCP stressed the importance of voluntary participation, incentives and rewards.

In 1953-54 a program of Agricultural Producers Cooperatives [APC] was launched. Initially the regime sought to develop "lower" APCs under unified management as a means of introducing the peasants to socialism. Voluntarism and the incentive principle were retained, and the peasants were to receive dividends for the shares of land, which they had contributed.

Mao's speech of July 1955, "On The Question of Agricultural Co-Operation" signaled an intensification of agricultural reform. In January 1956 the CCP announced that "lower" APCs had been fully developed and that the stage was set for the introduction of the principle of collectivization. This took the form of "higher" APCs in which the peasants would surrender their land; private ownership would not be permitted. The creation of each "higher" APC involved the amalgamation of several "lower" APCs, so that the boundaries of the former would coincide with the boundaries of a "natural village" of some one hundred households. Within two years, most Chinese peasants found themselves in "higher APCs.

The year 1958 marked the beginning of the "Great Leap Forward" in China's economic development and the further amalgamation of "higher" APCs into thousands of communes in which "collective ownership" was replaced with by "ownership by the people." A number of experimental communes were established quite early in the spring of 1958 but the official decision on the creation of the common system was not announced until late August. By fall, some twenty-six thousand communes were established throughout the country.

The Central Committee of the Chinese Communist Party approved a resolution on Establishment of People's Communes in the rural Areas in December 1958 with the following statement:

The people's communes are the logical result of the march of events. Large, comprehensive people's communes have made their appearance, and in several places they are already widespread. They have developed very rapidly in some areas. It is highly probable that there will soon be an upsurge in setting up people's communes throughout the country and the development is irresistible. The basis for the development of the people's communes is mainly the all-around, continuous leap forwarding China's agricultural production and the ever-rising political consciousness of the five hundred million peasants. The output of agricultural products has doubled or increased several fold, in some cases more than ten times or scores of times. This has further stimulated emancipation of thought among the people. Large-scale agricultural capital construction and the application of more advanced agricultural technique are making their demands on labor power. The growth of rural industry also demands the transfer of some manpower from agriculture. The demand for mechanization and electrification has become increasingly urgent in China's rural areas. Capital construction in agriculture and the struggle for bumper harvests involve large-scale co-operation, which cuts across the boundaries between co-operatives, townships and counties. The people have taken to organizing themselves along military lines, working with militancy, and leading a collective life, and this has raised the political consciousness of the five hundred million peasants still further. Community dining rooms, kindergartens, nurseries, sewing groups, barbershops, public baths, happy homes for the aged, agricultural middle schools, "Red and Expert" schools are leading the peasants toward a happier collective life and further fostering ideas of collectivism among the peasant masses. What all these things illustrate is that the agricultural co-operative with scores of families or several hundred families or several hundred families or several hundred families can no longer meet the needs of the changing situation. In the present circumstances, the establishment of people's communes with all-around management of agriculture, forestry, animal husbandry, side occupations and fishery, where industry [the worker], agriculture [the peasant], exchanger [the trader], culture and education [the student], and military affairs [the militia man], merge into one, is the fundamental policy to guide the peasants to accelerate socialist construction, complete the building of socialism ahead of time, and carry out the gradual transition to communism.

Changing the organization and size of the communes. Generally speaking, it is at present better to establish one commune to a township with the commune comprising about two thousand peasant households. Where a township embraces a vast area and is sparsely populated, more than one commune may be established, each with less than two thousand households. In some places, several townships may merge and form a single commune comprising six or seven thousand households, according to topographical conditions and the needs for the development of production. As to the establishment of communes of more than ten thousand or even more than twenty thousand households, we need not oppose them, but for the present we should not take the initiative to encourage them. As the people's communes grow there may be a tendency to form federations with the county as a unit. Plans should be drawn upright now on a county basis to insure rational distribution of people's communes.

Concerning the methods and steps to be adopted to merge small co-operatives into bigger ones and transform them into people's communes. The merger of small co-operatives into bigger ones and their transformation into people's communes is now a common mass demand. The poor and the lower-middle peasants firmly support it; most upper-middle peasants also favor it. We must rely on the poor and the lower-middle peasants and fully encourage the masses to air their views and argue it out, units the majority of the upper-middle peasants who favor it, overcome vacillation among the remainder, and expose and foil rumor mongering and sabotage by land-lord and rich-peasant elements, so that the mass of the peasants merge the smaller co-operatives into bigger ones and transform them into communes through ideological emancipation and on a voluntary basis, without any compulsion. As to the steps to be taken, it is of course better to complete the merger into bigger co-ops and their transformation into communes at once; but where this is not feasible, it can be done in two stages, with no compulsory or rash steps. In all counties, experiments should first be made in some selected areas and the experience gained should then be popularized gradually.

Concerning some questions of the economic policy involved in the merger of co-operatives. In the course of merger, education should be strengthened to prevent the growth of departmentalism among a few co-operatives, which might otherwise share out too much or all of their income and leave little or no common funds before the merger. On the other hand, it must be understood that agricultural co-operatives established on different foundations, the amount of their public property, their indebtedness inside and outside the co-operatives, and so on will not be completely equal when they merge into bigger co-operatives. In the course of the merger, the cadres and the masses should be educated in the spirit of communism so as to recognize these differences and not resort to minute squaring of accounts, insisting on equal shares and bothering with trifles.

When a people's commune is established, it is not necessary to deal with the questions of reserved private plots of land, scattered fruit trees, share funds, and so on in a great hurry; nor is it necessary to adopt clear-cut stipulations on these questions. Generally speaking, reserved private plots of land may perhaps be turned over to collective management in the course of the merger of co-operatives; scattered fruit trees, for the time being, may remain privately owned and be dealt with sometime later. Share funds, etc. can be handled after a year or two, since the funds will be automatically become publicly owned with the development of production, the increase in income, and the advance in the people's consciousness.

Concerning the name, ownership, and system of distribution of the communes. All the big merger co-operatives will be called people's communes. There is no need to change them into state owned farms, for it is not proper for farms to embrace industry, agriculture, exchange, culture and education, and military affairs at the same time.

After the establishment of people's communes, there is no need to immediately transform collective [state] ownership into ownership by the people as a whole. It is better at present to maintain collective ownership to avoid unnecessary complications arising in the course of the transformation of ownership. In fact, collective ownership in people's communes already contains some elements of ownership by the people as a whole. These elements will grow constantly in the course of the continuous development of people's communes and will gradually replace collective ownership. The transition from collective ownership to ownership by the people as a whole is a process, the completion of which may take less time; three to four years; in some places; and longer, five or six years or even longer elsewhere. Even with the completion of this transition, peoples communes, like state owned industry, are still socialist in character, where the principle of "from each according to his ability and to each according to his work" prevails. After a number of years, as the social product increases greatly, the communist consciousness and morality of the entire people are raised to a much higher degree, and universal education is instituted and developed, the difference between workers and peasants, town and country and mental and manual labor----legacies of the old society that have inevitably been carried over into the socialist period---and the remnants of unequal bourgeois rights, which are the reflection of these differences, will gradually vanish, and the function of the state will be limited to protecting the country from external aggression, but it will play no role internally. At that time Chinese society will enter the era of communism where the principle of "from each according to his ability and to each according to his needs" will be practiced.

After the establishment of people's communes, it is not necessary to hurry the change from the original system of distribution, in order to avoid any unfavorable effect on production. The system of distribution should be determined according to specific conditions. Where conditions permit, the shift to a wage system may be made. But where conditions are not yet ripe, the original system of payment according to workdays may be temporarily retained [such as the system of fixed targets for output, workdays and costs, with a part of the extra output as a reward; or the system of calculating workdays on the basis of output]. This can be changed when conditions permit.

Although ownership in the people's communes is still collective ownership and the system of distribution, either the wage system or payment according to workdays, is "to each according to his needs", the people's communes are the best form of organizational for the attainment of socialism and gradual transition to communism. They will develop into the basic social units in communist society.

At the present state the task is to build socialism. The primary purpose of establishing people's communes is to accelerate the speed of socialist construction and the purpose of building socialism is to prepare actively for the attainment of communism in China is no longer a remote future event. We should actively use the form of the people's communes to explore the practical road of transition to communism.

Each commune was intended as a self-sufficient economic, social and military unit. Special emphasis was placed on industrial development and back-yard blast furnaces studded the countryside. Communal kitchens, mess hall, nurseries, and schools were established. The basic family unit was weakened and women were placed in the center of production activity. The wage system was replaced by a combination of wages and "free supply" of food and clothing. An official slogan called for "more, better, faster, and more economical results."

The commune system involved widespread militarization by arming of the peasantry. Each commune was considered a unit of the people's militia. Production teams, production brigades, and production battalions were set up, closely resembling military organization. Commune members were awakened at dawn and marched off to work in military formations.

The commune system was intended to make possible more efficient utilization of labor, permit dispersion of population and industry [both important in case of war], and facilitate ideological remolding and Party control. The system as a whole was presented as a step toward the creation of a future communist society.

The commune enthusiasm did not last very long; by December 1958 it was already clear that communization had been premature and that the cadres had issued unwarranted and over-optimistic reports. The experiment had proved greatly wasteful of both resources and manpower; commune products were extremely poor in quality; some [e.g., back yard steel] were not only costly but literally unusable. Limitations in capital, resources, and technical and manageable skill forced a drastic slowdown. Production targets were revised downward by 50 percent or more, cadres were disciplined, and the regime popularized the "Red and Expert" slogan, stressing ideological commitment as well as technical proficiency. By August 1959 "higher" APCs had become fashionable once again. Two years later, the regime had turned all the way back to "lower" APCs and the peasants were allowed private plots of land. Thus began a three-year economic crisis in China, and it was exacerbated by the most serious natural disasters in many decades.

The failure of the commune system seemed to mark a personal setback for Mao Tse-tung. In December 1958, he resigned as CCP chairmanship, a position he had held simultaneously with his CCP chairmanship, nominally in order to devote his entire attention to Party and theoretical work. It now appears plausible that this resignation was more or less forced by Liu Shao-ch's [among others], who was named CPR chairman in April 1959. This incident may have played a significant role in the subsequent friction between the two men.

Soviet economic assistance to China [1950-60] was administered effectively and it laid the foundation for China's emergence as a world industrial power. Soviet aid for economic development amounted to about 2.5 billion dollars [a minor sum considering the fact that U.S. assistance to Taiwan has been at about the same level]. The USSR also provided thousands of technical advisors and substantial machinery and equipment.

China's First Five Year Plan [1953-57] emphasized industrial development, especially heavy industry [coal, steel, iron, electricity, petroleum, machine tools]. The Plan was primarily designed to strengthen the military and industrial base of China, with little attention to consumer goods. Most economic assets came under state control; most private firms were converted into joint state-private enterprises; most small businesses were reorganized into co-operatives.

The second Five-Year Plan [1958-62] involved little or no change from its predecessor. Industry continued to get most of the attention, although greater emphasis was placed on light industry. In the first year of the Second Plan, China sought to take a "leap forward" from agriculture backwards into industrial modernity. The announcement was formally made that China would surpass Great Britain in fifteen years. As the failure of the great leap became apparent, greater and greater emphasis was placed on agriculture. The slogan 'walking On Two Legs" stressed the simultaneous development of Agriculture and industry. Another slogan insisted that, "The whole party and the whole people go in for agriculture in a big way."

The early 1960's were years of economic recovery and consolidation in Communist China. Some segments of Chinese industry made a significant comeback, as shown by breakthroughs in nuclear technology since 1964. The third Five-Year Plan, which technically should have covered the 1963-67 period, was not announced until 1966. This plan stressed the simultaneous development of agriculture, heavy industry, and light industry.

CLASS STRUGGLE

Ideology provides a set of methodological tools for dialectical analysis. Although the Maoist ideology prescribes many analytical and practical methods, "one divides into two" [yi-fen-wei-erh] is probably the most sophisticated. This Marxist method of dialectical analysis was formulated for the socialist struggle against revisionist tendencies, following Mao's reassertion of effective ideological command at the Tenth Plenum of the Central Committee in 1962. Chou Yang, head of the CCP's Propaganda Department until the Cultural Revolution, gave the concept prominent play in his statement of October 26, 1963. According to the official CCP interpretation, the principle means that one must look at a person or a work from two sides, examining the good features, which should be no cause for complacency, and the deficiencies, whose correction demands unrelenting struggle.

For Mao, class struggle is a means of overcoming internal and external obstacles. Orthodox Marxist theory defined classes in relation to the material base of society and assumed that class struggle would no longer be necessary in the progressive society of socialism. Mao's new interpretation of the term is inward-directed in two senses: First, it is aimed against those among the party cadres and the working masses whose special privileges have made them a new class of "labor aristocracy" and, second, against any remaining influence of bourgeois ideology and undesirable traditions within each individual, regardless of his social background.

The establishment of a socialist economy is not enough for Mao; China must also be prosperous and strong, but without demanding too much of its resources. Mao is desirous of prolonging the revolutionary spirit beyond the socialist stage and postponing material incentives in the present by promising greater future rewards. Personal sacrifice will continue to be demanded. The Peking Review declared, "to abandon revolution on the pretext of avoiding sacrifices is a reality to demand that the people should forever remain slaves and endure infinite pain and sacrifice." Sacrifice at the present stage is thus presented as an investment in a millennial future; only by making sacrifices can a great future be assured.

Class struggle is not just directed toward the former ruling classes. It aims at three broad goals, all having direct relevance to the new value system. First, class struggle is employed to eliminate all rival centers of enculturation of the society, such as the family and the church, which may impart values opposed to those upheld by the Party's ideology. The family [or clan] system had inculcated particularistic values and pursued family –oriented interests, instead of the universalistic type of political and social order that the regime sought to establish.

The second broad goal of class struggle is to release peasants from all forms of "feudal" bondage in thought and in action, so that all productive forces can be freed. "The land ownership system of feudal exploitation by the landlord class shall be abolished", the Agrarian Reform Law declared, "and the system of peasant land ownership shall be introduced to set free the rural productive forces." Class struggle was more important to the Party that the actual improvement of peasant living standards, because the Party was willing to sacrifice immediate rewards for the present generation in order to increase productivity for the benefit of many generations to come. In Mao's view, class struggle rather than the immediate improvement of living standards is the only way to release and fully utilize all the latent productive forces. The People's Party stated in March 1963:

"The main demonstration of the class struggle and between the collective economy and the spontaneous Capitalist leanings of small producers. The surviving old ideas deeply ingrained in the minds of the peasant masses, and the habits and the customs left over from the old society cannot be wiped out overnight. The class struggle still remains in the countryside."

The third broad goal of class struggle is to overturn a value system that had traditionally regarded leisure and non-activity as superior to manual labor. Known as the shi-ta-fu his-ch'i or, literally, "the habit and aura of the gentry-literati", it was expressed in various ways an abhorrence of manual labor, a hypersensitive concern for "face", overt conformity but covert deviation, a dual standard of behavior toward in-groups and out-groups, outward geniality and internal suspiciousness, withdrawal from civic spirited activity, neglect for personal and public hygiene, and so forth.

Class struggle is a standard remedy for various tendencies the regime opposes. As a standing policy, the Party condemns inactivity as equivalent to opposition. The Maoists criticize "Lethargic mentality" because it leads to underestimating the enemy, indifference to class struggle, and apathy toward subversive actions, and also because it weakens the revolutionary ranks. At different times, the Maoist leadership has related "Lethargic mentality" to "rightist tendencies", "remnant capitalistic thinking", and "wanderers" among the youth who enjoyed new opportunities to travel and evade discipline and responsibility during the confusion of the Cultural Revolution.

Although Class struggle is a standard technique, the content of the term and targets of the regime have changed over time. Until about 1960, class struggle was an ideological struggle between classes, with the peasants and workers on one side and the bourgeois on the other. But, since 1960, bourgeois thought has been seen as an infection that contaminates all classes. Although in Mao's usage in the past class struggle did have the connotation of a struggle between conflicting ideologies as well as between the classes that generated them, the emphasis definitely shifted to the ideological aspect of the struggle in the 1960's. The new emphasis has arisen from the intra-party fight between Maoists and "revisionists." In current usage, the term means the struggle within each person, irrespective of his class background, between proletarian thinking and remnant bourgeois thinking. This new and quite unorthodox version of the Marxist concept may best be described as contrived class struggle.

Ideology sets up a body of concepts, terms, and ideas by which people interpret the world around them and communicate with one another. It serves to unify the thinking of the Party and the masses by establishing a uniform language for the discussion of national goals. A major vehicle for such communication is the Chinese press, whose function is not just propaganda or indoctrination but broad political communication.

The Chinese Communist leaders were trained to use the Marxist vocabulary, but the subconscious influence of Chinese thought probably persists. The leaders ostensibly use Marxist categories in their thinking and pronouncements and refer to economic interests, social classes, and class struggle. They claim that different class backgrounds determine individuals' responses to social issues. In "On People's Democratic Dictatorship," Mao Tse-tung stated: "Sun Yat-sen had a world outlook different from ours and started from a different class standpoint in studying and tackling problems.

Communication suffers from a somewhat distorted world view. The process of political communication in China is known as "Ideological work." By its doctrine of historical necessity and redemption, the Communist ideology has been transformed from academic speculation into an action program demanding positive commitment from its adherents. The Communist elite must not only mobilize itself, but it must also establish channels of political communication with the masses in order to mobilize the population at large.

In its ideological work, the Party must arouse the political consciousness of the nation and transmit its own aspirations, anxiety, and experience vertically to the masses and horizontally to the non-Party elites. Because the masses are so vast and because it is difficult to reform the thought of the thought of the non-Party elites [as the 1957 Hundred Flowers campaign demonstrated], the Party places a higher priority upon its vertical communications than upon its horizontal ones. Sensitively attuned to the importance of political communication, the Party seems to have always been seriously concerned with bridging the psychological and ideological distance between the Party and the public.

The Communist stress on political communication underlies the Party doctrine of the "mass line" [ch'un-chung luhsien]. The mass line is a broad statement of Party policy, expressed in ideological terms, and a principle of leadership and organization holding that Party cadres to the Party's must not merely proclaim their dedication to the Party's cause of serving the masses but must merge with the masses in a spirit of solidarity and lead them in implementing the Party's program. This is epitomized in the phrase, "From the masses, to the masses." Mao also regards the mass line as an indispensable means of furthering productivity.

Social integration, a central goal of the Chinese Communist Party, requires a unity of purpose, which a common vocabulary and system of thought can help create. The Maoists also believe that the process of political communication and social integration requires an unrelenting struggle to root out old and revisionist ideas, to purify the mind, and to remold humanity.

THE CULTURAL REVOLUTION

The Great Proletarian Cultural Revolution began in September 1965. Although it was a continuation of the more limited and unsuccessful campaign that Mao had waged since 1962 to uproot "poisonous weeks" in art and literature. At the outset, the Cultural Revolution was aimed at primarily the writers of influential literature, historians, university professor sand other intellectuals and performing artists.

The campaign of criticism and denunciation gradually spread to Party secretaries and propagandists, including the Minister of Culture, and eventually to top Chinese Communist Party leaders. The importance that Mao attaches to the cultural and ideological molding of men's minds is indicated in his charge that revisionism had penetrated every corner of the people's life.

The Cultural Revolution grew in intensity and violence and extended from central to peripheral issues. It does not seem to have followed any master plan. There was little logic to its series of spontaneous eruptions and its course of development suggests that Mao did not foresee certain specific events and features. He probably had no definite plan to remove some party leaders and no clear plan for the use of the Red Guards. He certainly did not intend to sanction the kind of anarchism that threatened to paralyze the entire nation until it was effectively curbed in 1968.

APPENDIX C

Comparative Systems

[Communism, Capitalism, and Socialism]

INTRODUCTION

Economic systems range from Capitalistic, through various stages of Socialistic to Communism. No one economy is purely one or the other, but all economies have adopted systems taking features from Capitalism and Socialism. The United States is the best example of Capitalism, the USSR is the best example of Socialism transformed into Communism, and Sweden is somewhere in between, but a good example of a Socialistic Society.

Socialism is defined as a theory of social organization based on government ownership, management or control of the means of producing and the production and exchange of goods.

Communism is a social organization in which goods are held in common. This theory advocates common ownership of means of production and an equal distribution of products of industry. It's base evolved from revolutionary Marxism socialism.

Capitalism is defined as an economic system characterized by private or corporate ownership of capital goods and by prices, production and distribution of goods that are determined mainly in a free market.

The purpose of this paper is to analyze representative samples of each system, and then perform a comparative analysis of the three systems.

ECONOMIC SYSTEMS
THE COMMUNIST SYSTEM [USSR]

The Soviet Union consists of 15 union republics, further divided into Republics, Regions and Areas. The highest organ of state power is the Supreme Soviet. The Communist Party with over 13 million members plays the leading role in Government and is the main policy making body. Military Service for 2 to 3 years is mandatory.

V. I. Lenin founded the Communist Party in 1903. In 1925, following the creation of the USSR, the All-union Communist Party of Bolsheviks was formed uniting various Communist Parties, and since 1952 has been called the Communist Party of the Soviet Union.

The Communist Party creatively developed the doctrine of Marxism-Leninism and proceeding from its principles seeks solutions to urgent problems arising in the course of building Communism.

The USSR, by Constitution, is a socialist state of workers and peasants, based on the philosophy of Karl Marx, and modified to the Communist principles of Lenin and Stalin. The economic foundation is the socialist system of economy and the socialist ownership of the instruments and means of production, firmly established as a result of abolishing the Capitalist system of economy, private ownership of the instruments and means of production and the exploitation of man by man. Socialist property in the USSR exists either in the form of state property or in the form of collective and cooperative farm property.

The economic life of the USSR is determined and guided by the State economic plan for increasing the wealth of society, and steadily raising the material and cultural standards of the working people and strengthening the independence of the USSR.

The economy is centrally planned based on public ownership and fits into the framework of a complete development plan. Economic planning was annually between 1919 and 1928. In 1929, Stalin introduced the Five-Year Plans.

Heavy industry accounts for more than two-thirds of the total industrial production. Industry has been the most important factor in the success of the economy since World War II. Accounting for more than 50 percent of the national income.

They have large-scale, mechanized agriculture with two types of farms. The collective farms work about half of the cultivated land, and distribute profits to members. The State farms are owned and operated by the State, the employees receiving wages.

The tax system provides the taxing of income by individuals, collective farms and cooperative societies. Individuals with income between 70 and 100m Rubles per month, pay 4.6 Rubles per month plus 12 percent over 70 Rubles. Those with 3 or more dependents are entitled to a 30 percent reduction. Childless persons 20 to 50 years old pay 6 percent of their total income. Collective farms and citizens that hold plots for personal use average paying .85 Rubles per .01 hectare [2.47 acres] tax. Internal trade is conducted by State trading establishments, consumers' cooperatives and collective farm markets. Foreign trade is a State monopoly.

Between 1960 and 1970, National income rose by 41 percent, industrial production by 50 percent, and real income increased by one-third. The Five-Year Plan for 1971-75 envisioned another 30 percent increase in real incomes. For the first time the production of consumer goods surpassed that of capital goods. A 41-45 percent growth was planned for Capital goods and a growth of 44-48 percent was planned for consumer goods. National income was planned to grow by 37-40 percent and agricultural output by 20-22 percent.

Since 1966 industry has been implementing an economic reform broadening the business initiative of enterprises and strengthening the role of economic incentives. Between 1973 and 1975, a new system of management was introduced to increase the flexibility and efficiency of management, involving a radical reorganization of ministries and their chief departments.

In 1973 the state allocated over 27 million Rubles for social insurance and maintenance. Also, they have a complete range of social security benefits, such as disability pensions, loss of breadwinner, student grants, maternity benefits; and pensions are paid to retired men at 60 and women at 55. This retirement pay averages 60 to 70 percent of their salary prior to their retirement. Employees in enterprises where the work is arduous may receive pensions 5 or 10 years earlier. In 1972 there were 42 million retired persons.

A new social security scheme for old and disabled collective farm workers has been implemented. This is financed by deductions from the farmer's wage made by the collective farm, and of allocations from the State Budget. In 1973, one-third raised disability pensions with greater material assistance to families with children, and benefits for working mothers were raised.

They have a streamlined system of public health services providing medical aid for the entire population. All medical services and treatments are free as well as drugs and medicines in hospitals. Most sanitariums and holiday homes are under jurisdiction of trade unions. Accommodations for children and all persons in tuberculosis sanitariums are free. Working people pay about 30 % of the cost. Workers temporarily unable to work because of sickness receive a sick leave benefit by certificate issued by the adult polyclinic. Disabled workers are either transferred to lighter work or put on disability pension. The 1971-75 Five-Year Plan increased spending on social welfare by 40 percent.

The National Economic Plan, 1961-1980 contains the following:

Increase industrial productivity by 300-500 percent.

Total electrification of the country expansion of the metals and fuels industry, Development of Automation, Development of Jet Engineering, Rationalization of the distribution of industry, Entire electrification of agriculture, Higher .pay for better work and greater material incentives , and Higher efficiency of collective farms.

THE CAPITALISTIC SYSTEM
[UNITED STATES OF AMERICA]

The United States is the best example, if not the only, of Capitalism in the world today. It is based on a democratic free-enterprise system with minimum government control. It is a world leader in nearly all branches of production and trade, greatly exceeding that of any other country. The economy is based on private ownership and entrepreneurship, with minimum government interference.

The U.S. economic system was not originally fashioned after any particular model. However, it does represent a system, and possesses or should possess the following chief elements:

Vigorous competition.

Freeenterprise.

Profit motive.

A freely operating price system.

Vigorous competition is the striving to gain an advantage over rivals. In business, it is making strenuous efforts to gain customers at the expense of others, and to grow while they decline. Competition takes place from senior executives down, individuals striving to defeat competitive firms and win promotions for themselves within the firm over colleagues.

Free enterprise is offering the individual the right to engage in any business activity, with no fields reserved either to government or to selected individuals.

The profit motive is the key goal of business as the making of money gains in private investment.

The price system is not only the most complex of U.S. economy elements it is the most fundamental. The basic rationale for an economy based on competition, free enterprise, and the profit motive id found in the logic of a price system.

Industrial activity is divided into three sectors, large corporation, individualist, and government. Large corporations are basically dictatorial organizations and owned by private investment. They yield great social power, significant political power, and are sometimes classified as inefficient. However, the large firm has contributed greatly to increased efficiency in production and helped to speed technological improvement.

The individualist, or small business sector has become a steadily less important member of U.S. economy although he remains a significant factor both economically and socially.

The Government sector represents several layers of government involved in U.S. economy. This is by far the largest single factor in the economy, and is concerned primarily with its nature and activities. It is also a very large customer for corporations and individual businesses.

Agriculture is a competitive, free enterprise activity, although it is affected by other economic elements, and subject to some government controls. It can be further divided into large scale and family farm levels, which determine their own means of production, capital expenditures, marketing, and distribution of profits.

The tax system provides federal, state, and local taxation on income, property and inheritance. These taxes are levied on corporations, individuals and all profit groups. There are many tax schedules and special deductions for various groups. As an example a majority of persons earning over one million dollars per year, they pay little or no tax due to several "tax shelters" or "tax loopholes" as referred by some. The main element supporting the country the economy through taxation is the middle-income group.

Internal trade is conducted purely by private enterprise. Some government control is performed to prevent fraud, tax evasion and conflict of interest. Foreign trade is conducted by private enterprise although the government controls import-export quotas, export of strategic or sensitive materials, regulates import taxes, assists private investment in developing foreign markets and performs other controls to protect the U.S. economy.

The capitalist processes of the U.S. have resulted in a constant increase in national income, industrial production, and agricultural production. This has created a standard of living unequalled anywhere in the world. This system is highly oriented toward services, with 63.6 percent of the economic active population. Industry accounted for 32.7 percent and agriculture accounted for 3.7 percent. The lower percentages in industry and agriculture are results of technical advances necessitating more services and less employment in agriculture and industry. The U.S., like most other countries has been faced with an increasing deficit in balance of payments, increasing inflation, and growing unemployment.

Social welfare and insurance programs consume a moderate percentage of government spending when compared to other countries. These programs are mainly oriented toward the aged, unemployed, and low-income groups. The largest federal program is Social Security which provides retirement for self-employed and workers, disabled, and minor children of deceased. This is partially paid for through income deductions. The U.S.has not yet implemented a complete public health service system, although government assistance is utilized for many local health services, mainly oriented toward better health services for the poor and underprivileged.

The U.S. does what may be termed as tentative economic planning. The Council of Economic Advisors studies economic developments closely and forecasts levels of business activity. It advises the President and provides information to Government officials and to the business community on what is happening and what can be expected. However, no individual business or labor union is compelled to take or forego actions to improve economic conditions.

Labor unions play a very important part in the U.S. economy. They are not controlled by any government agency and have the power to close certain segments in their demands for higher wages, more security and better working conditions. In instances of a complete impasse between the union and industry, federal mediators are sometimes called upon to mediate differences and develop a suitable solution.

THE SOCIALIST SYSTEN (SWEDEN)

The government is a hereditary Monarchy as a result of the Constitution of the Kingdom of Sweden, dating from 1809. However, it operates on a democratic and parliamentary basis. The principal political party is the Social Democratic Party, representing 43.6 percent of votes. Others have lesser percent representation, with the Communist Party having 5.3 percent. The State controls the Church of Sweden, of the Evangelical Lutheran faith, with the King required to profess the pure Evangelical creed.

Also, the State controls all church property. About 95 percent of the population are members.

Sweden's popular image is the prototype it has provided for a modern welfare state, a "middle way" which is socialist but non-communist. However, their standard of living is exceeded only by the United States.

The 1973 death of King Gustaf VI, who had ruled since 1950, and the accession of Carl XVI Gustaf permitted a new constitution to come into force in 1975, reducing the monarch's role to that of a ceremonial head of state, and creating more power by the Social Democratic Labour Party.

Sweden is one of the member founders of the European Free Trade Association [EFTA] but has not applied to join the European Economic Community [EEC] commonly referred as the Common Market. They consider that joining the EEC might compromise Swedish neutrality and affect the security of the Swedish farmers, although favoring the reduction of trade barriers.

Exports make up over 20 percent of the GNP, which is the highest per capita in Europe.

The government encourages small farms to pool their machinery, and nearly every farmer is a member of the producer's cooperative for marketing agricultural products. However 90 percent of the arable land is privately owned and not more than 20 percent is held in lease. The principle intent of the Swedish agricultural policy is to further the creation of larger cooperative units.

Production of power and goods contribute about 50 percent of the GNP, representing only a slight rise. Manufacturing is the major factor, with agricultural and fishing shares declining. Public services, trade, transportation and communication top the list of services.

About 8 percent of the working population are in agriculture, forestry and fisheries, producing about 3 percent of Sweden's GNP. In 1972, 29 percent of the working population was in manufacturing industry consisting mainly of metalworking and engineering. Next significant, slightly less than 29 percent was community, social and personal services.

Sweden enjoys the highest average income in Europe, more than the U.S., at $4600 per person in 1972, but the people are subject to very heavy taxation to pay for comprehensive social welfare policies. Many businesses are State owned, grouped in a State holding company which is one of the largest industrial concerns.

Ninety percent of Swedish industry is privately owned. Cooperative enterprises account for about 5 percent and about 5 percent is publicly owned either by State or local authorities. The more important publicly owned industries are consolidated under a State corporation. Role of government is not extensive in direct management of industrial or business enterprise.

They have long been a leader in social welfare. Compulsory health insurance programs reimburse most doctor's fees, hospital treatment and medicines. A national pension system is paid to all citizens over 67 years of age, and to foreign residents in Sweden who have resided there for a designated period of time. In addition, a supplementary pension based on average yearly income will be paid in full to all persons born after 1914.

There is a highly advanced system of social security programs covering old age and family pensions, sickness, unemployment, and disability benefits based on a National Pension Fund. Expenditures on the social services consume a considerable part of the national income. In late 1969, the State took over the pharmaceutical industry as part of Health Socialization.

A large percentage of the GNP goes into the public sector in the form of taxes and social charges, and much is returned to the private sector through insurance payments of different kinds. Taxes and social charges constitute over 40 percent of the GNP, the largest of any nation. About one-third of this money returns to mainly private households.

About one-fourth of the GNP finances public activities, about one-half to local authorities. Most of this money is returned to the citizens in the form of services of which education, health, defense and welfare are the largest.

Taxes are charged partly as a strong progressive national income tax including a local proportional income tax, tax on net wealth, and inheritance and gift tax. In addition, taxes are levied on business profit, as are indirect taxes such as the value-added tax. Tax on corporations is about 50 percent of net profits in addition to a tax on dividends to stockholders.

Children allowances are paid for each child under 16, and every mother receives a stipend at each childbirth. Unemployment insurance is based on voluntary premiums but subsidized by the State. Between 1965 and 1970, state expenditures for social security doubled

The average household consists of 3 persons. Less than one-half reside in individual houses. They spend an average of 17 percent of their income on housing. About one-half of the housing is privately owned, about one-fourth by housing cooperatives, and the remainder by semi-public bodies. Private ownership has fallen sharply mainly due to inequity in State assistance for housing. Private builders get 85 percent State loans whereas cooperatives and semi-public bodies receive 95 to 100 percent.

They have the most highly organized unions in the world. About 80 percent of all wage earners belong to a trade union. The Swedish labor market has always been regarded as peaceful, with a good mutual understanding between employers and employees, with a tradition of negotiation that has guaranteed proper functioning of agreements. The unions were recently put on par with management in running companies, with right of access to all information, including company secrets and full negotiation rights in agreements and related matters and matters of production methods.

Heavy consumption of imported oil and slackening export orders produced a $1.2 billion shortfall in 1975 and required borrowing abroad to compensate for a growing Balance of Payments deficit. Balance of Payments deficit is presently $2.17 billion.

The current plan is to ride out the recession by maintaining high employment and priming industry for an upswing in 1976. The mid-year 1975 budget released $1.93 billion to assist industry and provided$482 million to assist industrial investment through guarantees for loans and tax relief.

APPENDIX D

Managenent Subversion

Management Subversion has been a little known activity for more than 30 years in the Military and Corporate areas. The following was taken from a paper titled, "Research in Organizational Theory", dated October 1970. It was distributed at the Army Command and Staff College, taught by the Army; and civilian Executive Seminars taught by the Civil Service Commission In this group of subversion techniques, the emphasis is placed upon work-related methods. This involves the normal day-to-day organizational operations, and is most easily implemented by a superior manager.

Give him too much work. This involves the piling on of excessive legitimate work, well beyond the capabilities of a normal manager. Care must be taken that the work asked for is managerial and cannot be delegated downwards. If there is even a remote chance of accomplishing all the extra work, double it. This is particularly effective if the work is under outside scrutiny or is due by some well-known deadline date.

Take away most of his work. The goal with this technique is to insure that all work assigned can be accomplished in a few minutes every day. This technique can be implemented in a multitude of very mechanical ways, such as deleting certain reports due, reassignment of the work to another group, not assigning any new jobs, etc. The goal of this technique is to undermine the individual's sense of purpose within the organization.

Nit-pick his correspondence. Refuse to pass any correspondence until it is letter perfect. It is particularly aggravating to change sentences and sentence structures so that it's meaning is warped. If any correspondence does not get through unscathed, deliberately redline a sentence and write your own comments in red and initial the comments.

Delay his correspondence. Do not even read what he writes, nor pay any attention to it. Do nothing, and especially do not pass it on. If information copies have been distributed before you signed the correspondence, call them all back.

Borrow his best people. This technique can disrupt the entire group under the manager's control. Assign his best people to "crash jobs" outside of his control. Do not ask permission first, just do it, and tell him about it. This is particularly effective if his best people have established personal relationships with the manager.

Low merit raises or salary reviews. According to the pay scale, deliberately give the man a raise low enough to be considered an insult. This can be accompanied with a completely bland performance review.

Request fast-response status reports. Every once in awhile, ask for a detailed status report on Friday afternoon, due Monday morning. This should be sufficiently detailed to force the man to work over the weekend and disrupt any plans he may have had.

Override his decisions. This should be done sporadically, calling your shots. This can be more effective if the decision involves work that the manager had spent considerable effort completing and one in which he is deeply involved.

Company security violation. Giving the man's secretary a "company restricted" piece of mail, unmarked as such, late in the afternoon, can set this up. The first thing next morning, conduct a department wide search for the letter and discover it in his in-basket. Do not take any other action, but make sure he knows where the letter was found.

Deny or ignore material requisitions. Do not approve any requisitions for supplies, office equipment, or services. Tell him to "make do." If there is justification for the equipment or material, tell him to "borrow it."

Assign work beneath him. This technique demeans the man. Assign him work considerably below his capabilities, and force the man to do it himself. Examples of this method are; manpower histories, checking sick leave requests, etc.

Assign the man an assistant. Give him an assistant to "ease his work-load." Over a period of time, deliberately task the assistant, talk to him, and generally upgrade the assistant's informal authority. Make sure the manager knows the assistance is "one of your men."

Go into excruciating detail. Every time the manager asks for help or gives status reports, get deeply into the detail of what he is doing. Question the reasoning behind each decision made. Make it apparent that his performance is under constant scrutiny.

Send the man on useless trips. If he dislikes to travel, make sure the trips are complex, difficult to conduct, and are frequent enough to keep him off balance. Recruiting trips to college campuses are a good example. Suggest that he not take his family along. It is even possible to force the man to run up his traveling expenses, beyond that which is reasonable for reimbursement. Travel to northern areas in winter can be particularly exasperating.

Stop the man's traveling. This is only effective if the manager is used to frequent traveling, and it is part of his normal job. Suggest that he send somebody else for the really important trips.

Question his judgment. In staff meetings, especially, cast doubts about his decision-making ability. Make it obvious that although you will go along with him that you do not agree. If this technique is implemented in the office, make sure his subordinates are within earshot. The objective here is to plant the idea that you do not trust his judgment.

Suspend his bonus. If the manager is receiving a managerial-level incentive bonus, temporarily suspend this benefit for any trivial reason. This is a direct confrontation over basics, so be prepared to justify your reasons.

Cut off the informal flow of information. Much of the day-to-day work involves your informal discussions with your subordinates. Deliberately cut the manager off from this source. Make it a point to discuss things in staff meetings, which you did not discuss with the manager previously. This will be most effective on topics, which are not important, so that the chance of his knowing about them through other sources is slim.

Force him to miss staff meetings. If the staff meetings can be scheduled so that you occasionally have them without his presence, the informal transfer of information [see immediately above] can be slowed down.

Assign him a doomed project. Give him work that is destined to failure. This should not be applied to a real go-getter, as he might pull the fat out of the fire and become a department "hero". Assign this onerous work with suggestions that it doesn't really matter if he louses things up, they can't get much worse.

POLITICAL TECHNIQUE

This section covers those factors, which can be arbitrarily assigned as political in nature. These involve the continuing jockeying for position that is always going on in any organizational climate. In general, office politics is concerned with the enhancement of a person's status, both informally and formally. There are no rules to obey in office politics, and almost anything goes. An adroit office politician can significantly influence much of the formal work that any department does. If a superior-subordinate relationship does exist, then a superior manager has a distinct advantage politically, over the subordinate. We can use the authority of his office to back up politically motivated actions.

Office politics is not a game for amateurs. It consists of give-and-take, compromise, and the swift realization of personal opportunity. If the manager, upon which politically orientated strategies are being applied, in an entrenched office politician then the job of removing him by subterfuge will be particularly difficult. In this respect, the victim can use counter-strategies against his superior manager. If the subordinate manager is dull and uncomprehending of political nuances, much of what follows may be a waste of time. The blatancy of the application of politics is dependant upon the particular situation.

Change the performance rating of the manager's subordinates. If he submits a vertically –ordered list of the people in his department, based on his evaluation of their performance, deliberately change the ranking just enough to cast doubt on his ability to assess other people.

Don't invite him to all your staff meetings. Deliberately omit an invitation to routine meetings. If you are aware of a request for his presence at outside meetings, go in his place. Do this often enough to jar the continuity of control he may exercise.

Open criticism. This should be done in public, in front of other people, preferably his subordinates. Gentle hints of your discontent are usually enough to set a department buzzing. This technique should be differentiated from a continuous needling on performance. The object here is to reduce the respect his department may have for him.

Violation of line authority. Every once in awhile, deliberately go around him on some mundane technical matter. Go right to his subordinates. Do not bother to inform him, of the fact, even after-the-fact. Any technical information picked up in this manner can be used later as a club in your hands, especially if he is trying to cover something up.

Borrow his secretary. This is especially effective if his secretary has been with him for a long time. The ultimate blow would be to replace her with an incompetent girl. Borrowing his secretary for periods of time long enough to disrupt his office routine is best. If this can be time- phased during known periods of heavy secretarial workloads, all to the best.

Promote one of his subordinates without his prior knowledge. This will have the effect of frustrating any ranking procedures he may have in effect. If you can take advantage of any personal conflicts within his department, this ploy will be traumatic.

Force him to take vacation prematurely. This can be prefaced with a forecasted crash job or some other pretext. A corollary to this would be to force a last minute cancellation of vacation plans.

Get him involved in an unsolvable personal problem. From department history, is should be easy to determine where personnel conflicts exist. Sending the manager in to settle long-standing disputes should rekindle old hatreds. This type of intervention can only be interpreted as meddling, so the manager cannot solve anything. A particularly good opportunity might develop if the manager takes sides.

Force him to take a stand on a union issue and then back away. This can be most effective if the issue is not clear. Let him interpret company policy and enact it, then offer grudging support, complaining that you have been forced to compromise company policy because of a subordinate's actions. If the issue gets to the grievance state, a forum is already prepared to demean your subordinate.

Load his department with troublemakers. If you have the authority to maneuver the people under you, a gradual shifting of the known troublemakers into the manager's department will make life miserable for him. A normal manager cannot, effectively control troublemakers such as union radicals, religious zealots, psychological problems, etc. This ploy will lay the groundwork for future internal problems within his group.

Use his prejudices against him. If the manager has a few particular personal prejudices, these can be effectively used to precipitate obvious blunders on his part. As an example, assign him the task of performing a detailed study into some technical or managerial area about which you know he has pre-conceived ideas. Unless he is usually objective, his personal feelings will become part of the study effort. These feelings can be used as clubs against him to discredit the study effort.

Cut back his group until he is over-managing. This can be done by directing a personnel layoff in his group, without his concurrence, to the point where his group rebels at the increased workload and increased meddling into individual job situations on his part. Requests for transfers should also increase under conditions such as this. The result will be frustration.

Bring in a watchdog group to look over his shoulder. In most companies, there is some form of management auditing or value analysis group, which is charged with the responsibility of evaluating departmental performance. The presence of outside interference such as this is unnerving. The very point that you brought the outside group in is indicative that you are dissatisfied with performance. The danger in this approach lies in the fact that spin-off from any audit might detract from your managerial problems in his group, this could be damaging to you.

Withhold managerial privileges. This technique affronts the status symbology system in force. Good examples are the withholding of prime parking privileges, withholding new office appurtenances, not having his office painted, etc.

Confide specific information to his secretary and not to him. This is particularly effective if the information is policy related or has to do with personal work. What is desired here is that he will "get the word" from his secretary and not directly from you. This will enhance his secretary's prestige at the cost of his. This will also trigger the grapevine and announce via the informal organization structure that you are dissatisfied with his performance.

Make an obvious display of your interest in his work. Keep his internal records on your desk. Make it obvious to him that he is being evaluated continually. This might be used at times of the year when there is no apparent reason for this interest, just after a pay raise was issued, for instance.

Repetitive development interviews. This is similar to the above, but is different in the fact that you are constantly harping on his managerial deficiencies. This is a heavy-handed way of alerting him to your displeasure. Intangibles are amenable to this technique, such as union relations, initiative, etc.

Accuse him of being unethical. If there is any cause for doubt about a particular decision he has made, accuse him of unethical conduct. This strikes directly at his moral fiber. Of course, if the entire organization is basically unethical, this technique is of no value.

Frequent office moves. Move his department or his office around enough to disrupt his normal functioning. The chaos resulting from frequent moves can result in sub-standard performance. This technique can be augmented with frequent telephone number changes, which effectively cut him off from routine communication channels. If the size of the office is a status symbol, this can be juggled accordingly.

Set up an ethnic problem for which a known prejudice exists. This technique employs his own weaknesses to discredit him Examples are numerous. If he is a hard-core southerner, for instance, force him to work with [or for] colored people. Religious prejudices can also be used in the same way. These types of situations are ugly, and the unfortunate part is that any dire consequences might rub off on you.

CPSIA information can be obtained at www.ICGtesting.com
Printed in the USA
LVOW111950280911

248241LV00002B/95/P